The Autobiography

of

Gemma Galgani

{and her diary}

HAGIOS PUBLICATIONS

2020

S. GEMMA GALGANI   (vera fotografia)

A Prayer *of* Gemma *to* Jesus

O my crucified God, behold me at Your feet; do not cast me out, now that I appear before You as a sinner. I have offended You exceedingly in the past, my Jesus, but it shall be so no longer. Before You, O Lord, I place all my sins; I have now considered Your own sufferings and see how great is the worth of that Precious Blood that flows from Your veins. O my God, at this hour close Your eyes to my want of merit, and since You have been pleased to die for my sins, grant me forgiveness for them all, that I may no longer feel the burden of my sins, for this burden, dear Jesus, oppresses me beyond measure. Assist me, my Jesus, for I desire to become good whatsoever it may cost; take away, destroy, utterly root out all that You find in me contrary to Your holy will. At the same time, I pray to You Lord Jesus, to enlighten me that I may be able to walk in Your holy light.

Foreword

Gemma Galgani is a mystic, a visionary, a prophet, and, above all of those things, a lover of Jesus—one of his prized daughters. When her heart burned after taking Holy Communion, was this a real physical sensation? *Yes*. When she prayed for lost souls, weeping for them even if she barely knew them or didn't know them at all, was she fully convinced, with no doubt in her mind, that they would be saved? *Yes*. When she spent time with her Guardian Angel, and with Mary, and with Jesus, she does tell us that all of these events are in her mind, but what is she really saying? That she is insane, or that a mystic cannot (and does not wish to) differentiate between this world we so erroneously call 'reality' and the real Life we like to call Heaven? The latter is true, of course. This editor bears witness to her truth, able to corroborate with like experiences—and also different ones—since he was a small child.

We begin this book here in the foreword with a *short anonymous biography* of Gemma Galgani, after which is included a *prayer* of Gemma to Jesus. We follow with the *diary* of Gemma, then continue with her *autobiography* commissioned by her Father-Confessor Germanus Ruoppolo and later stolen by a demon, scorched with fire, and only returned when the venerable man, stationed four hundred miles away from the village of Lucca, performed a rite of exorcism which forced the devil to return the book to Gemma. We conclude these pages with a *longer anonymous biography* of Gemma.

†

Gemma Galgani, called the 'Flower of Lucca,' was an Italian mystic also often referred to as the 'Daughter of Passion' for her intense replication of the Passion of Christ.

She was born on March 12, 1878, in a small Italian town near Lucca.

At a very young age, Gemma developed a love for prayer. She made her First Communion on June 17, 1887.[1] As a student at a school run by the Sisters of St. Zita, Gemma was loved by her teachers and her fellow students. Though quiet and reserved, she always had a smile for everyone. Gemma, though, had to quit school due to her chronic ill health before completing her course of study.

Throughout her life, Gemma was to be chosen[2] for many mystical experiences[3] and special graces.[4] These were often misunderstood by others, causing ridicule. She suffered heartaches in reparation, remembering that Our Lord Himself had been misunderstood and ridiculed.

Gemma had an immense love for the poor and helped them in any way she could. After her father's death, the 19-year-old Gemma became the mother-figure for her seven brothers and sisters. When some of her siblings became old enough to share the responsibility, Gemma went to live briefly with a married aunt.

At this time, two young men proposed marriage to her. Gemma refused because she wanted silence, retirement, and more than ever, she desired to pray, and to speak only to God.

Gemma returned home and almost immediately became ill with meningitis. Throughout her illness, her one regret was the trouble she caused her relatives who took care of her. Feeling herself tempted by the Devil, Gemma prayed

---

[1] By special permission, since she was about three years too young according to Catholic custom.

[2] by God

[3] Such as numerous visions of her conversing with Jesus, Mary, and her Guardian Angel.

[4] One of these graces being the highly unusual 'burning' of the heart and chest area upon receiving the Body and Blood of Our Lord in Holy Communion.

for help to the Venerable Passionist, Gabriel Possenti. Through his intercession, she was miraculously cured.

Gemma wished to become a nun, but her poor health prevented her from being accepted. She offered this disappointment to God as a sacrifice.

Gemma predicted that the Passionists would establish a monastery at Lucca; this came to pass two years after her death. Today, Gemma's relics remain at the Passionist monastery in Lucca.

On June 8, 1899, Gemma received an internal warning that some unusual grace was to be granted to her. She felt pain, and then blood issued from her hands, feet, and heart. These were the marks of the *stigmata*. Each Thursday evening, Gemma would fall into rapture and the marks would appear. Such marks are the appearance of the wounds of the Crucified Jesus on the bodies of some men and women whose lives are so conformed to His that they reflect those wounds of His redemptive love for others.

Her stigmata would remain until Friday afternoon or Saturday morning. Then the bleeding would stop, the wounds would close, and only white marks would remain in place of the deep gashes. Gemma's stigmata would continue to appear until her Confessor, Reverend Germanus Ruoppolo, advised her to pray for their disappearance due to her declining health. Through her prayers, the phenomenon ceased, but the white marks remained on her skin until her death.

Through the help of her Confessor, Gemma went off to live with another family where she was allowed more freedom for her spiritual life than when she was at home. There, she was frequently found in a state of ecstasy and on one occasion she was believed to have levitated. Her words spoken during her ecstasies were recorded by her Confessor and a relative from her adoptive family.

At the end of her ecstasies, she would return to normal and carry on quietly and serenely. Gemma often saw her

Guardian Angel. She sent her Guardian Angel on errands, usually to deliver a letter or oral message to her Confessor in Rome.

During the apostolic investigations into her life, all witnesses testified that there was no artfulness in Gemma's manner. Her severe penances and sacrifices were hidden from most who knew her.

In January of 1903, Gemma was diagnosed with tuberculosis. At the start of Holy Week in 1903, Gemma began to suffer greatly. She died at age 25 on Holy Saturday, April 11. The Parish Priest in her company said, 'She died with a smile which remained upon her lips, so that I could not convince myself that she was really dead.'

St. Gemma Galgani was beatified[1] on May 14, 1933 by Pope Pius XI and canonized on May 2, 1940, only 37 years after her death, by Pope Pius XII. Her feast day is celebrated on April 11.

---

[1] In the Roman Catholic tradition, this is the first step toward being recognized as a saint (canonized).

The Diary *of* Gemma Galgani

[English translator unknown; parenthetical notations belong to
Gemma; footnoted by the publisher]

Diary Part 1

July 1900

Thursday, July 19

This evening at last, after six days of absence of Jesus,
since it was Thursday, I began my hour of prayer,[1] thinking
of Jesus on the Cross. Then it happened. I found myself
with Him suffering and I felt a great desire to suffer and
asked Jesus to give me this grace. He granted it; He
approached me, took from His head the crown of thorns
and placed it upon mine, and then went aside. I looked at
Him silently, for I was thinking perhaps He did not love me
anymore, because He had not pressed the crown down hard
upon my head as He had done at other times. Jesus
understood and pressed it upon my temples. They were
painful but happy moments. I then spent an hour with
Jesus. I should have liked to continue with Him thus all
night, but Jesus loves obedience very much; He Himself
always submits to obedience, so when the hour was up He
left me. Generally Jesus took the crown off when He was
leaving; this time, however, He left it until about four
o'clock the following afternoon.

---

[1] Gemma made a holy hour every Thursday evening, since her
miraculous cure, something she had promised to do. She made this holy
hour every Thursday until her death.

Friday, July 20

By four o'clock today I was tired of suffering. I presently found myself with Jesus, Who came beside me and was not sad as on the previous night; He caressed me and lifted the crown from my head. I then felt less pain; but when He put it upon His own head I felt no pain at all. My strength returned and I felt even better than before I began to suffer.

We talked of many things, and during our conversation I asked Him not to make me confess to Father Vallini, because I did not like to. Jesus seemed disappointed, and told me that I should go at once. I promised I would. He showed His heart to me and said 'I love you greatly because you are like me.'

'In what way, Jesus?' I asked, 'because I seem so unlike you.'

'In accepting humiliations,' He replied. Then there returned to me a vision of my past life. I saw my pride. It was always one of my greatest defects. When I was little, wherever I went I always heard it said that I was very proud. But what means Jesus has used to humiliate me, especially during this past year! At last I understand what God was doing with me. May Jesus be always thanked. Then God added that with time He would make a saint of me. Of this last I will say no more, for that is impossible to happen to me. He told me of something to say to the Confessor and blessed me. I knew Jesus would be away from me for some days. But how good He is! Scarcely had He gone when my Angel Guardian appeared, who with his continual charity,[1] vigilance, and patience assists me. Oh Jesus, I have promised always to obey You. I affirm it anew.

---

[1] love

2

Saturday, July 21

My dearest Mother of Sorrows[1] came to pay me a little visit as she is accustomed to on Saturday.

She seemed very unhappy and looked as if she had been weeping. Then she smiled, saying to me:

'Gemma, do you wish to repose on my breast?'[2] I approached her and knelt; she raised me, kissed me on the forehead and disappeared.

This evening, after confessing to Father Vallini, I felt suddenly agitated and disturbed; it was a sign that the Devil was near. Later, internally and also externally, I was all in a tempest; I should have preferred to go to bed and sleep rather than to pray, but no, I began to say three invocations, which I usually say every evening to the Sacred Heart of Mary. The enemy, who had been hidden for some hours, appeared in the form of a very small man, but so horrible that I was almost overcome with fear.

Continuing to pray, all at once I began to feel many blows on the shoulder which continued for about half an hour. Then my Angel Guardian came and asked me what the matter was; I begged him to stay with me all night, and he said to me, 'But I must sleep.'

'No,' I replied, 'Angels of Jesus do not sleep.'

'Nevertheless,' he replied, smiling, 'I ought to rest. Where shall you put me?' I begged him to remain near me.

I went to bed; after that he seemed to spread his wings and come over my head. In the morning he was still there.

---

[1] Mary, mother of Jesus
[2] i.e. 'Gemma, do you want me to hold you?'

Sunday, July 22

The Devil, in the form of a great black dog, put his paws upon my shoulders, making every bone in my body ache. At times I believed that he would mangle me; then one time, when I was taking Holy Water, he twisted my arm so cruelly that I fell to the earth in great pain.

After a while I remembered that I had around my neck the relic of the Holy Cross.[1] Making the Sign of the Cross, I became calm. Jesus let me see Himself, but only for a short time, and He strengthened me anew to suffer and struggle.[2]

At dinner time, there had come to me an evil thought which my Angel understood and he said to me 'Daughter, do you wish me to go away?' I was ashamed. These words I heard very distinctly and I did not know whether or not others also heard him.

While in church yesterday, he reprimanded me, saying: 'The glory of Jesus and the place where you are merit another kind of conduct,' because at that time I had raised my eyes to look at two children, to see how they were dressed.

Last night, while in bed, he reproved me again, saying that instead of progressing in his teachings I was becoming constantly worse and continually slackening in well-doing.

I am always conscious when these things happen to me. It seems to me that no matter what I do, I do not succeed in preparing myself for the visit of the Mother of Sorrows or Brother Gabriel.[3]

---

[1] A piece of the Cross of Jesus.
[2] 'Take up your cross, and follow me.'
[3] Saint Gabriel Possenti

4

I went to bed, I slept, and slept well; after a quarter of an hour, for my sleep is always brief, I saw at the foot of my bed, on the ground, that usual ominous black creature, very black, very small. I knew who it was and said, 'Have you begun again the business of not letting me sleep?'

'What, sleep? Why don't you pray?' he replied.

'I shall pray later,' I said. 'Now it is time to sleep.'

'For two days you have not been able to be recollected; well, let's do what I want.' He began to give me blows, until he jumped up suddenly and rolled on the ground. I do not know what happened, but I smiled, for I did not have any fear of him today.

He said, 'Today I can do nothing to you, but I'll take care of you another time.'

I asked him: 'Why can't you? If you can do it other times, why can't you now? I know I am the same, but I have Jesus (the relic) on my neck.'

Then he said to me: 'What have you in this room? Take off the belt[1] (Saint Gabriel's) you wear and then we shall see.'

I insisted that I had nothing, but I knew what he meant. After this, I smiled at him as he stood there devoured with rage. He told me that if I prayed I would suffer all the more.

'It doesn't matter,' I said. 'I suffer for Jesus.'

In short, today I was much entertained by him.[2] I saw him very angry; he has sworn to make me pay for it.

He waited until this evening, but by the grace of God he was not able to remain very long; he gave me three violent blows so that afterward going to bed took much time. At

---

[1] St Gabriel Possenti had, recently in a vision, given Gemma his belt that the Passionists wear.

[2] i.e. 'The demon spent much of the day with me.'

certain times he ran off and with such fear that I did not know what the matter was.

I myself was scarcely able to move.

How often I called Jesus! But He did not come; I prayed that my Angel Guardian should lead me to Jesus, but everything was in vain. He said to me: 'Tonight Jesus will not come to bless you, nor will I.'

I was frightened then, because if Jesus did not bless me I could not get up— he saw that I was about to weep and said: 'But you know, Jesus will send someone. And if you knew who it was, how happy you would be.'

My mind flew at once to Brother Gabriel. I asked him, but he made no reply; he kept me in suspense for some time. At last he said to me: 'But if Jesus does send Brother Gabriel to bless you, what will you do? Do not speak to him if you do not want to disobey the Confessor.'

'No, I will not speak,' I replied impatiently, 'but how can Brother Gabriel bless me?'

'It is Jesus who sends him; he has sent him other times to bless you. But will you manage to be silent and obey?'

'Yes, yes, I will obey; let him come.'

After a little while Brother Gabriel came. What a frenzy seized me then! I wanted to speak to him, but I was good and checked myself.[1] He blessed me with certain Latin words which I have remembered well, and then he suddenly departed. Oh, then I could not help saying: 'Brother Gabriel, ask our Mother to bring you to me Saturday.' He turned to me smiling and said:

'You are to be good,' and saying this took from his waist his black belt and said 'Do you want it again?'

I wanted it very much indeed: 'That helps me so much when you let me wear it; please give it to me now.' He shook his head to indicate that he would give it to me

---

[1] During this period, St Gemma's Confessor, Monsignor Volpi, had ordered Gemma not to speak to any of the persons in her visions, although she was allowed to speak to her Angel.

6

Saturday, and left me. He told me that the belt was the one which had liberated me from the devil[1] the night before.

It happened today as usual. I had gone to bed, in fact I was asleep, but the devil did not wish this. He presented himself in a disgusting manner; he tempted me but I was strong. I commended myself to Jesus asking that He take my life rather than have me offend Him. What horrible temptations those were! All displease me but those against Holy Purity make me most wretched. Afterward he left me in peace and the Angel Guardian came and assured me that I had not done anything wrong. I complained somewhat, because I wished his help at such times, and he said that whether I saw him or not, he would be always above my head. Also, yesterday he promised that in the evening Jesus would come to see me.

Yesterday evening I waited with impatience for the moment to go to my room; I took the crucifix and went to bed. My Angel was willing to have me go to bed because of the order of the Confessor.[2] I felt myself becoming recollected. Jesus came and stood by my side. What beautiful moments

---

[1] demon

[2] Gemma's Father-Confessor is also her spiritual guide concerned about her spiritual state and mental health and therefore forbidding her to speak to any persons she sees in her visions or mystic revelations. She obviously cannot find it within herself to obey, but this inclination is apparently overlooked by those who visit her as well as her Confessor (to some extent). One is reminded of the teaching of John of the Cross where he forbids not only conversations but any meditation at all on visions or mystical experiences, pointing always to a life filled with blind trust and the spiritual consolations brought by Jesus as we live united with Him in a deep love relationship as his Bride. This teaching is, of course, merely foundational (yet very important), as one remembers the observation of C. S. Lewis when he writes that those who live lives of holiness in the Body of Christ are like branches on a large and spreading tree—and the more we reach up into the sky and spread (the more saintly we become) the less we are seen (understood) by the other branches which, of course, are still part of the tree (Body of Christ).

those were!

I asked Him if He would love me always, and He replied with these words: 'My daughter, I have enriched you with so many beautiful things without any merit on your part and you ask Me if I love you? I fear so much for you.'

'Why?' I asked.

'Oh daughter, on the days when you enjoy My presence you are all fervor, it costs you no fatigue to pray. Now instead you are wearied by prayer, and negligence in your duties seeks to insinuate itself in your heart. Oh daughter, why do you speak thus? Tell me, in the past, did prayer seem long as it does now? Some little penance you do, but how long you wait before resolving upon it.'

Finally I commended His poor sinner to Him.[1] He blessed me and in going away said to me:

'Remember that I have created you for Heaven; you have nothing to do with the Earth.'

†

---

[1] She rededicates her life to Jesus.

Diary Part 2

Last of July/Early August 1900

Wednesday, July 25

And what about today? What shall I say today? I find no peace; pride predominates over me more than in earlier times. I suffer much to complete even a small act of humiliation. About what happened to me yesterday I shall speak very little; I do not control my tongue, and for this reason I cause other people to suffer.

For obedience to my Confessor, I must speak very little and never with people who know about my experiences. A few days ago, when Father Norberto came, I hid instantly; another time he came and I did the same; I was ready, truth be said, to be obedient, but then what happened to me? After a few days I chanced to be speaking to another friar[1] about this and I invented a big lie, saying that it was Mrs. Cecilia who had made me hide; but that was not true, it was I who did it on my own.

I don't know how Father Norberto came to learn of this, but instantly he referred the matter to Mrs. Cecilia, who was very hurt. But I was no less hurt. She interrogated me about whether I had really spoken and I answered no, because I had completely forgotten about it; but there's always the one who makes me remember everything; my Guardian Angel came and reproached me, saying:

'Gemma, what's this, even lying? Don't you remember a few days ago, when, as punishment for telling Brother Famiano about your experiences, I made you stay half an hour?'

I then recalled everything well (I must say that my

---

[1] monastic brother

9

Guardian Angel, every time I do a bad thing, punishes me; not an evening passes that I do not have some punishment), and he commanded me to go to Mrs. Cecilia and tell everything and beg her in his name to forgive me.

I promised to do this, sure! The day passed, then came the evening and I never made that little act of humility. My angel reminded me again, saying that if I didn't go to her and tell her everything, that night the Devil would come.

Well, that threat I could not ignore, and so I went to her room. She was in bed and the lamp was out; I couldn't believe it: this way she would not see me. As well as I could, I told her everything, but in a forced way; it was a great shame, my being unable to humiliate myself. Finally, after she said all would be forgotten, I went to my room. Yes, of course! She said all was forgotten, but it was impossible. I asked Jesus many times for forgiveness and also my beloved angel, and I went to bed. What a horrible night! My angel, because of the great resistance I had put up before accepting my humiliation, left me alone, and with a few visits by the enemy. I could not sleep because my conscience was ill at ease; how I was troubled!

Thursday, July 26

In the morning, my Guardian Angel finally came, and he reproached me harshly, very harshly and left me once again alone and afflicted. I received Communion[1] but, my God, in what a state! Jesus did not make Himself felt. When after all this I was able to be alone, then I let out my feelings freely; I was at fault, I realize that; but if I can say one thing, I did not wish to cause certain displeasures to certain persons, but my evil inclinations are so bad that I often fall into these things. For more than an hour Jesus made me

---

[1] The Eucharist ('Good Divine Favor') or the Body and Blood of Jesus (i.e. His Presence).

10

stay in that state; I cried, and I was afflicted. Then Jesus had pity on me and He came; He caressed me and made me promise not to do these things again, and He blessed me.

I have to say that in what happened yesterday, I told three lies, I had angry thoughts, and I had the idea of avenging myself against whoever had tattled on me, but Jesus prohibited me from speaking with Brother Famiano and with others. I quickly became calm, and to be even more so, I ran to confession.

Then in the evening, after saying my prayers, I set out to do the usual Holy Hour prayer. Jesus stayed with me throughout; I was in bed,[1] as usual, because otherwise I would not have been able to remain with my beloved Jesus and suffer with Him. I suffered a lot; He proved anew His love toward me by giving me His crown of thorns until the following day; Jesus loves me most on Friday. That evening He took back the crown, saying He was happy with me, and, as He caressed me, He said: 'Daughter, if I add other crosses, do not be afflicted.' I promised, and He left me.

Friday, July 27

This Friday I suffered even more, because I had to do some chores and at every moment I thought I would die. Indeed, my aunt had commanded me to fetch water: I felt so exhausted I thought the thorns went into my brain (but this was all my imagination), and a drop of blood began to appear at my temple. I hurriedly cleaned up so she barely noticed it. She asked me if maybe I had fallen and cut my head; I told her that I had scratched myself with the chain from the well. Then I went to the nuns, it was 10:00 a.m.

---

[1] During this period, Gemma's Confessor Monsignor Volpi had ordered Gemma to go to bed in the evening, and not linger in her room in prayer.

and I stayed with them until about 5:00 p.m. Then I returned home, but Jesus already had removed the crown.

Saturday, July 28

The night passed very well; in the morning my Guardian Angel came; he was happy and he told me to take a piece of paper and write what he would dictate. Here it is:

'Remember, my daughter, that whoever truly loves Jesus speaks little and bears everything. I order you, on behalf of Jesus, not to give your opinion unless you are asked; never to hold to your own wishes, but to submit immediately. Obey promptly your Confessor and others he designates, without answering back; when it is necessary, make only one reply, and be sincere with your Confessor and with others. When you have committed some fault of omission, accuse yourself instantly, without waiting to be asked. Finally, remember to guard your eyes, and think—eyes that have been mortified will see the beauty of Heaven.'

After saying these things, he blessed me and said I should go to Communion. I went right away; it was the first time in nearly a month that Jesus had made Himself felt.

I told Him all of what was happening, and He kept me with him a long while, because I received Communion at 8:30 a.m. and when I returned to my senses it was much later. I ran home and on the way the clock struck 10:15 a.m. I was good and found myself in the same position that I had been in during Communion, and as I got up I saw that my Guardian Angel was above my head with his wings spread. He accompanied me home himself and warned me not to pray during the day, not until nightfall, because I could not be safe. In fact I realized that I was safe from the others in the household, but not from my sister, because she had stuffed the keyhole and it was impossible to lock myself in; then my aunts intervened and in the evening I could close the door.

Toward evening, I went to the Fifteen Saturdays at St Maria Bianca[1]; the Blessed Virgin told me she would not be paying me her usual little visit because in the past few days I had disgusted Jesus. I said to Her that Jesus had forgiven me, but she said:

'I don't forgive my daughters so easily; I absolutely want you to become perfect: we'll see if Saturday I can come and bring Brother Gabriel.'

Nevertheless, she blessed me, and I resigned myself.[2]

But I do not lack for temptation; one, a strong one, was Saturday evening: the Devil came and said to me: 'Good, good girl! Sure, go and write everything: don't you know that everything you write is my work, and if you are discovered, think about the scandal! Where will you go to

---

[1] The parish church of the Giannini family.

[2] Of course Mary forgives easily, as do all celestial beings found beneath the Kingship of Jesus. But here Mary is using a ruse in order to help Gemma understand the depth of her transgressions. Is this a lie from Mary, even if it is a 'white lie'? The only fair answer is that a *true* lie is one that harms and does not heal. Mary knows how to use the 'white lie' for Gemma's benefit. (We must remember that Jesus was once asked if he was going up (the mountain) to Jerusalem, and he replied that he would not be going, only to later go in disguise.) Suppose a mother wants her little girl to eat spinach pies because of the health benefits, but the child isn't fond of the 'green' taste. So, the mother pretends to be angry, saying that she spent much time preparing the pies and so a lack of gratitude is not right. She knows already that this method will make her daughter feel sad and want to be grateful for what she has in life. Is this mother lying, or only using the classic 'white lie' in order to help her daughter be healthy until such time as she can make her own decisions about what she eats? So it is with Mary and her alleged 'unforgiveness.' Gemma, as we see, is affected in a positive way.

hide? I pass you off as a saint, but you are deluded.'

I felt so badly that, out of desperation, I swore that when Mrs. Cecilia returned I would destroy what I had written. In the meantime, I tried to tear this writing up but I couldn't; I didn't have the strength, or else I just don't know what happened.

Sunday, July 29

I remained in this state until yesterday morning, Sunday, without being able to collect myself; my Guardian Angel, however, does not leave me: he gives me strength, and I must say that Sunday I had no appetite, but he himself ordered me to eat, as he did today also. Every evening he did not fail to bless me, but also to punish me and yell at me.

Today, Sunday, I feel a great need for Jesus, but it is already late and I no longer have any hope; I expect to spend the night free and alone.

But Jesus came, you know! How He reproached me because I had not gone to Communion. This is how Jesus reproached me: 'Why, oh daughter, am I so often deprived of your visits? You know how much I yearn for you to come to Me when you are good.'

I fell on my knees in front of Jesus and in tears I said: 'But how can this be, my Jesus? Aren't You tired of putting up with me and all my coldness?'

'Daughter,' He answered. 'See to it that from now on not a day goes by without your coming to Me; try to keep your heart pure and adorned with every possible care.[1] Drive all self-love away from your heart, and anything else that is not entirely Mine, and then come to Me without fear.'

He blessed me, along with all the members of the *Sacro*

---

[1] adorned…care = made beautiful with every possible discipline

14

Collegio;[1] and went away; indeed, in the end He advised me to have a little more strength in combating the enemy, telling me to take no account of those words because the Devil is always a liar who seeks every means to make me fall, especially about obedience. 'Obey, My daughter,' he repeated. 'Obey instantly and cheerfully, and to achieve victory in this beautiful virtue, pray to My mother[2] who loves you so much.'

I would have wanted to tell Him that yesterday His mother didn't wish to come, but He disappeared.[3]

Monday, July 30

This morning I went to Communion. I did not want to: I was not at peace with my conscience; I lingered until 9:00 a.m., thinking if I should go or not; then Jesus won and I went to Communion, but how? With what coldness! I was completely unable to feel Jesus.

Today I was not able to collect myself at all; I was bad, I got angry, but only by myself, no one else saw me: I cried so, so much, because my sister Angelina did not want to leave my room. Yesterday evening, Sunday, for spite, she stayed in my room until 11:00 p.m., making fun of me, saying that she wanted to see me go in ecstasy; today again the same thing. She wrote a letter yesterday to Bagni di S.

---

[1] *Sacred College*; the body of all Cardinals of the Roman Catholic church. God works with each of us individually. Jesus knew that the Cardinals and Pope were important to Gemma, and so He blessed them all for Gemma's sake. For a Baptist in Alabama, He may bless the local pastor and his fellow ministers since Cardinals and Popes mean little or nothing to most Protestants.

[2] i.e. ask my mother (Mary) for her prayers

[3] Had Gemma told Jesus, would He have been surprised? This journey from the world of sin to Heaven (and all that idea holds) is all about the change of our perceptions from earthly to heavenly. Jesus and His saints know this, having once been on Earth, and work with us accordingly—and individually.

Giuliano[1] and spoke a lot about me and my experiences. These things, which I should be accepting happily and with thanks to Jesus, instead upset me, and I almost have moments of despair.

While I was in that state, my Guardian Angel, who was watching me, said: 'Why are you so upset, my daughter? You have to suffer something, you know, for Jesus.' (In truth, what displeased me most were certain words that my sister had said out loud to me), and to this my angel responded: 'You are worthy only to be scorned, because you have offended Jesus.' Then he calmed me, sat at my side, and said gently, very gently: 'Oh daughter, don't you know that you must conform in every way to the life of Jesus? He suffered so much for you, don't you know that you must on every occasion suffer for him? Furthermore, why do you give this displeasure to Jesus, of neglecting to meditate on his Passion every day?'

It was true: I recalled that I did a meditation on the Passion only on Fridays and Thursdays.

'You must do it every day, remember that.' Finally, he said to me: 'Be brave, be brave! This world is not a place for rest: rest will come after death; for now you must suffer, and suffer all things, to save some soul from eternal death.'

I begged him urgently to ask my Mother[2] to come to me a little, because I had so many things to tell her, and he said yes. But this evening she did not come.

Tuesday, July 31

We are at Tuesday; I run to Communion but in what a state! I promised Jesus to be good and to change my life; I said it, but He didn't answer anything; I also asked that He

---

[1] Baths of Saint Giuliano, where most likely were priests to minister to those who visit for healing.
[2] Mary

send his Mother, and also mine,[1] and He responded: 'Are you worthy?' I was ashamed, and I said nothing more. Then He added: 'Be good and soon she will come with Brother Gabriel.'

It's been since Sunday that I have been unable to collect myself; nonetheless I thanked Jesus. When my Guardian Angel comes, I am awake, and my head does not take off; Jesus, my Mom[2] and sometimes Brother Gabriel make my head take off; but I always stay where I am; I always find myself in the same place, it's just that my head departs. What a great need I have for my Mother! If Jesus would grant me this, afterward I would be better. How am I supposed to go so long without Mom?

Wednesday & Thursday, August 1st & 2nd

Wednesday, I could not collect myself at all. Nor Thursday; from time to time my Guardian Angel would say something to me, but I was always awake; in fact, Wednesday evening, interiorly I thought I might be deceived by the Devil; my Guardian Angel calmed me by saying: 'Obedience.'

Now coming to Thursday. As usual, out of obedience I went to bed; I began my prayers and immediately collected myself. For a while I had been feeling ill. I stayed all alone; when I was suffering, Jesus wasn't there, and I suffered only in my head. My Confessor asked me this morning if I had experienced the signs, and I said no. They hurt a lot, but not compared to my head. Poor Jesus! He made me stay alone for about an hour, but then He came and showed up like this, all bloodied, saying: 'I am the Jesus of Father Germano.' I did not believe him, and you know why.[3] I am

---

[1] Here she reaffirms to herself that Mary is also her mother.

[2] The familiar form of Mother, for Mary.

[3] Gemma is referring to the Devil, thinking that maybe her visitor is not really Jesus.

always fearful, always. I pronounced these words: 'Long live Jesus and Mary'[1] and then I understood. He gave me a bit of strength but internally I was still afraid, and He said: 'Do not fear: I am the Jesus of Father Germano.'[2] He urged me of His own free will, without my even suggesting it, to pray for Mother Maria Teresa of the Infant Jesus[3] because she is in Purgatory and suffering greatly. Jesus wants her quickly with Him, I think.[4]

Friday, August 3

Today I slept a little, then I felt completely collected; after becoming collected I felt my head take off: I was with Jesus. How happy I was! Yes, I suffered so much in my head; I complained a little because He is leaving me alone. I begged Him also to tell me when Mother Maria Teresa would be in Heaven. He said: 'Not yet; she's still suffering.' I commended my poor sinner[5] to Him and He blessed me and all the members of the *Sacro Collegio*, and He left me in a happy state.

   This evening I felt I could not collect myself; I said a few evening prayers and went to bed. To tell the truth, I foresaw a bit of a storm because Jesus had warned me a few days ago, saying: 'The enemy will try you with one final battle, but it will be the last because now that is enough.' I could not help but thank Him for the strength He

---

[1] 'Lunga vita a Gesù e Maria.' (Italian)

[2] Gemma had not yet met Father Germano, although Jesus had shown him to her in a vision and told her that he would someday be her spiritual director.

[3] 1825-1889, Foundress of the Congregation of the Sisters of Our Lady of Carmel

[4] Here we see evidence that Gemma, whether she really knows it or not, has developed a deep and abiding relationship with Jesus, so much so that she feels free to interpret how Jesus is feeling about things—a sign of great friendship. Here we also see co-creation with Jesus at work.

[5] Maria Teresa

had always given me, and I prayed that He would want to give me strength for this final test as well, that is to say, last night.

I went to bed, as you know well, with the intention of sleeping; slumber was not long in coming when almost instantly a tiny, tiny man appeared, all covered in black hair. What a fright! He put his hands on my bed and I thought he wanted to hit me: 'No, no,' he said. 'I am not able to hit you, don't be afraid,' and as he said this he lay down on the bed.

I called Jesus to help me but He did not come, but this doesn't mean He abandoned me. As soon as I called His name I felt liberated, but it was sudden.

Other times I had called Jesus but He had never been ready like last night.

You should have seen the demon afterward, how angry! He rolled around on the floor, cursing; he made one last effort to take away the cross I had with me, but then he instantly fell backward.

How good Jesus was with me last night. The devil, after that last effort, turned toward me and said that since he had not been able to do anything, he wished to torment me the rest of the night.

'No,' I told him; I called my Guardian Angel, who opened his wings and alighted next to me; he blessed me and the bad devil[1] ran away. Jesus be thanked.

This morning I learned that at the very moment the devil was rising in fury, the scapular of Our Lady of Sorrows had been placed on me[2] and I realized that when the devil was trying to take something off of me, it could be nothing but that. My Mother, Our Lady of Sorrows, also be thanked.

---

[1] A common noun meaning 'demon.'
[2] by Cecilia Giannini

Saturday, August 4

Here I am at Saturday: it's the day destined for me to see my Mom,[1] but should I hope for it?

Finally evening has arrived. I set out to recite the Sorrowful Mysteries of the Rosary; at first I abandoned myself, that is to say, I placed myself in God's will, to spend that Saturday also without seeing Our Lady of Sorrows; but for Jesus this offering was enough of a sacrifice and He fulfilled my wishes. At some point, I'm not sure where in the rosary, I felt completely collected, and with this collection, as usual, quickly my head took off, and without realizing it, I found myself (it seemed to me) in front of Our Lady of Sorrows.

Upon first seeing her, I was a little afraid; I did all I could to assure myself that it was truly Jesus' mother, and she gave me every sign to assure me. After a few moments I felt entirely happy, but I was so moved by seeing myself, so little compared to her, and so content, that I could not say a word except to repeat the name 'Mom'.

She stared, really stared, at me, laughing, and approached to caress me, and she said I should calm down. Yes, of course, happiness and emotion grew in me, and she, maybe fearing that it would be bad for me (as happened other times, indeed one time, which I did not tell about, when for the great consolation I felt in seeing Jesus again, my heart started beating with such force that I was obliged, on the orders of my Confessor, to tie a tight, tight bandage around that point), left me, saying that I should go and rest. I obeyed promptly, and in one second I was in bed and she did not delay her coming; then I was calm.

I also must say that upon first seeing these things, these figures (that certainly could have been deceptions), I am initially taken with fear; then fear is followed quickly by

---

[1] Mary

joy. However that may be, this is what happens to me. I spoke with her about some of my desires, the most important one being that she should bring me with her to Heaven; this I said to her several times. She answered: 'Daughter, you must suffer still more.'

'I will suffer up there,' I wanted to say. 'In Heaven.'

'Oh no,' was her reply. 'In Heaven there is no more suffering; but I will bring you there very soon,' she said.

She was near my bed, so beautiful, I contemplated her and could not get enough. I commended my sinner[1] to her; she smiled: that was a good sign. I further commended to her various persons who were dear to me, in particular those to whom I have a big debt of gratitude. And this I had to do also on the order of my Confessor, who last time beseeched me to commend them fervently to Our Lady of Sorrows, saying that I could do nothing for them but that the Blessed Virgin may ask on my behalf and bestow on them every grace.

I feared that she would leave me at any moment, and so I called her repeatedly and said she should take me with her. Her presence made me forget about my protector, Brother Gabriel. I asked about him, why hadn't she brought him along, and she said: 'Because Brother Gabriel demands more exact obedience from you.' She had something to tell me for Father Germano; to these last words she did not answer.

While we were talking together she constantly held my hand, and then she let go; I did not want her to go and I was about to cry; then she said: 'My daughter, that's enough; Jesus wants this sacrifice from you, now it's time for me to leave you.'

Her words calmed me and I answered with tranquility: 'So be it, the sacrifice is done.'

---

[1] Possibly Mother Maria Teresa.

She left. Who could describe precisely how beautiful, how beloved is the Heavenly Mother? No, for certain there is no comparison. When will I have the good fortune of seeing her again?

†

Diary Part 3

August 1900

Sunday, August 5, 1900

Today, Sunday, I prayed to my Guardian Angel to grant me the favor of going to tell Jesus that I would not be able to do a meditation because I did not feel well; I would do it that evening. But that evening I had no desire; I went to bed and made preparations for meditation, but collected myself only internally. My head did not take off; I stayed this way for an hour. Indeed, I should add that the Sunday meditation is always on the Resurrection, actually on Heaven; but Jesus makes it clearly known to me that He does not wish me to do that meditation just yet, because my mind immediately rushes to some principal point in His Passion. Let His will be done.

Monday, August 6

Here I am at August 6th. The days pass and here I am always in the same worldly abyss.

This evening my Guardian Angel, while I was saying evening prayers, approached me and, tapping me on the shoulder, he said: 'Gemma, why such disinclination for prayer? This distresses Jesus.'

'No,' I answered, 'it's not disinclination: but for two days I have not been feeling well.'

He responded: 'Do your duty with diligence and you shall see that Jesus will love you even more.' For a moment he was silent and then he asked: 'And Brother Gabriel?'

'I don't know.'

'How long is it that you haven't seen him?'[1]

'A long, long, long while.'

'Then tonight Jesus will send him.'

'Really? Tonight no, I would be disobeying: at night my Confessor is opposed.' Oh with how much desire I would have wanted him! but I also wanted to obey. I prayed to send him in the daytime and soon, so that I could write that letter to Father Germano. I urged my Guardian Angel to go to Jesus and ask permission to spend the night together with me. He immediately disappeared.

I had finished prayers: I went to bed. When he[2] had gotten permission from Jesus to come, he returned; he asked me: 'How long has it been since you last prayed for the souls in Purgatory? Oh my daughter, you think of them so little! Mother Maria Teresa is still suffering, you know?' It was since morning that I had not prayed for them. He said he would like me to dedicate every little pain I suffered to the souls in Purgatory. 'Every little penance gives them relief; even yesterday and today, if you had offered a little for them.'

I answered with a bit of astonishment: 'My body was hurting; and do bodily pains relieve the souls in Purgatory?'

'Yes,' he said. 'Yes, daughter: even the smallest suffering gives relief.' So I promised that from that moment onward I would offer everything for them. He added: 'How much those souls suffer! Would you like to do something for them tonight? Do you want to suffer?'

'Doing what?' I said. 'Is it the same suffering Jesus did on Good Friday?'

'No,' he answered. 'These are not Jesus' pains; yours will be bodily pains.'[3]

---

[1] Saint Gabriel Possenti

[2] her Guardian Angel

[3] Here we are given some insight into the sufferings of Jesus—that they were not physical or bodily.

I said no, because except for Thursday and Friday Jesus does not want this; the other nights He wants me to sleep. But since the souls in Purgatory, and in particular Mother Maria Teresa, are so dear to my heart, I told him I would gladly suffer for an hour.

These words satisfied him, but he saw clearly that in doing so I would have been disobedient, so he let me sleep.

This morning, when I awoke, he was still beside me; he blessed me and went away.

Tuesday, August 7

During the day yesterday my Guardian Angel promised me that in the evening I would be able to speak with Brother Gabriel. The long-awaited evening arrived; in the beginning I was sleepy, then an agitation came over me, enough to frighten me. But since Jesus was about to grant me this consolation, either before or after the consolation, He gives me some suffering. Jesus be always blessed.

Still, in undergoing this agitation I saw no one, I mean the devil; it's just that I felt very ill, but it lasted only a short while. Quickly I calmed down; suddenly I felt completely collected and then almost immediately it happened like usual; my head took off and I found myself with Brother Gabriel. What a consolation that was! For obedience I was not allowed to kiss his vestment and I restrained myself.[1] The first thing I did was ask him why he had stayed so long without visiting me. He answered that it was my fault. Of this I was sure because I am very bad. How many beautiful things he told me about the convent and he said them with such force that it seemed to me his eyes sparkled.

---

[1] Obedience to her Confessor who at that time ordered her not to touch any of the heavenly visitors.

On his own, without my asking: 'Daughter, within a few months, amidst the exultation of almost all Catholics, the new convent will be founded.'

'What do you mean, in a few months?' I said, 'if there are still 13 months to go.'

'That's a few,' he responded. Then, smiling, he turned to one side and knelt, clasped his hands and said: 'Blessed Virgin, look: here on Earth is the competition for propagating the new institute; come on, I beg you, make the abundance of celestial gifts and favors shower on all those who take part. Increase their strength, increase their zeal. It will be entirely your gift, oh Blessed Virgin.'

He talked as if Our Lady of Sorrows were next to him; I could see nothing, but with such force, with such expression did he say those words that I remained amazed; it seemed like his head also had taken off.

Now I should speak about Father Germano, but my Confessor said no, because—

I also spoke of my poor sinner;[1] he smiled, always a good sign. Finally he left me filled with consolation.

Wednesday, August 8

Now we come to this morning. A little while after leaving the confessional, a thought came to me; thinking to myself that my Confessor made too little of my sins, I was disturbed. To calm me down, my Guardian Angel approached; I was in church, and he pronounced these words out loud: 'But tell me, who do you want to believe, your Confessor or your head? Your Confessor, who has continuous light and assistance, who is highly capable, or else yourself, who has nothing, nothing, nothing of all this? Oh what pride!' he said. 'You want to become the teacher,

---

[1] Possibly Mother Maria Teresa, then in Purgatory. Gemma was always beseeching her heavenly visitors for the conversion of some soul or another. She called them 'my poor sinners.'

26

guide, and director of your Confessor!' I did not think further; I made an Act of Contrition and then went to Holy Communion.

Thursday, August 9

Today also, after having sustained with the help of God a battle with the enemy, a very strong one, my Guardian Angel came reproaching me, and with great severity said: 'Daughter, remember that in failing in any obedience, you always commit a sin. Why are you so reluctant in obeying your Confessor? Remember also, there is no shorter or truer path than the one of obedience.'[1]

So why all this today? It was my fault. I would deserve even worse, but Jesus always shows me mercy.

Alas, what disgust I experience this evening! Since early morning I have felt so tired, but it's all laziness, bad will; still I want to overcome it, with the help of God.

It is Thursday and therefore I feel very strange; on Thursday evenings I always feel this way. Yes, suffer, suffer for sinners, and particularly for the poor souls in Purgatory, and in particular for— And I know well why this laziness so early in the day. The other evenings it came upon me a few hours later. It was because today my Guardian Angel told me that tonight Jesus wanted me to suffer a few extra hours, precisely two hours: at 9:00 p.m. it would begin, for the souls in Purgatory, and without my Confessor's permission; but usually he does not yell at me, indeed he wishes it, and I am free to do it. Last night, around 9:00 p.m., I began to feel a little ill; I was quick to bed, but I had been suffering already for a while: my head ached beyond measure and any movement I made caused

---

[1] Obedience to those who are, without any doubt, godly; but there is a great danger in obedience to merely anyone who carries authority within organized religion because more often than not their power is misused.

me terrible distress. I suffered for two hours, as Jesus wished, for Mother Maria Teresa; then with great pain I undressed and got into bed and began to pray. It was very painful but in Jesus' company one would do anything!

Friday, August 10

My Guardian Angel said the previous evening that I was allowed to keep the thorns in my head until 5:00 in the afternoon on Friday; it was true, because around that time I began to collect myself completely; I hid myself in the Franciscan church and there Jesus came to me again to remove them; I was alone the whole time. How He showed me that He loved me! He encouraged me anew to suffer and he left me in a sea of consolation. But I must say that many times, in particular on Thursday evenings, I am overcome with such sadness at the thought of having committed so many sins, they all come back to me: I am ashamed of myself, and I feel afflicted, so afflicted. Even last night, a few hours earlier, this shame came over me, this grief, and I find a little peace only in that bit of suffering Jesus sends me, offering it first for sinners, and in particular for me, and then for the souls in Purgatory. How many consolations Jesus gives me! In how many ways He shows me his love! They are all things of my head; but if I obey, Jesus will not permit me to be deceived. Thursday evening He promised that in these days when Mrs. Cecilia was away, He would not leave me without my Guardian Angel. He gave me the Angel last night and from then on he[1] has not left me for even a moment.

This I have observed many times, and I have not spoken of it even with my Confessor, but today I tell all. When I am with other people, my Guardian Angel never leaves me;

---

[1] the angel

however, when I am with her,[1] the angel immediately leaves me (I mean to say that he does not show himself anymore, except to give me some warnings); the same thing happened today: he never left my side for a minute; if I have to speak, to pray, to do something, he lets me know. May Jesus not allow me to be deceived.

This thing so astounds me that it obliged me to ask of him: 'How is it that when Mrs. Cecilia is with me, you never stay around?'

He answered like this: 'No person, other than she, knows how to take my place. Poor girl,' he added, 'you are so little that you always need a guide! Fear not, for now I shall do it, but obey, you know, because I could easily—'

I went to confession; I told this to my Confessor (I had also written to him about it); so he explained what I did not understand, so now I understand everything.

Saturday, August 11

It's Saturday; I'm going to Holy Communion. What shall I do? Whatever, I shall obey. If only I could obtain a little visit from my Mom. But no, I remember the sin I committed last night. It's true that this morning I confessed myself immediately, but alas, the Blessed Virgin does not forgive so easily, especially with me.[2] She wants me to be perfect.

It's Saturday evening, my God! What punishment! It's the biggest punishment you can give me, depriving me of a

---

[1] Cecilia Giannini

[2] Mary pretends sternness because she doesn't want Gemma to give herself any slack in discipline, prayer, and suffering on her own cross for others. This seems strange, but each saint is worked with on an individual basis with his or her personal blueprint. There are no paper-doll cutouts in Heaven.

29

visit from Most Holy Mary, and it's precisely around Saturday that I always fall into many omissions.[1]

Sunday, August 12

Sunday has arrived. What indifference, what dryness! Still, I do not want to abandon my usual prayers.

Wednesday, August 15
  Feast of the Assumption of Mary into Heaven

I remained in this state of dryness and the absence of Jesus until today, Wednesday. Since Friday I've heard nothing. My Confessor assures me this is a punishment for my sins or to see if I can stay without Jesus, and to stimulate me to love him more.[2] I have been alone throughout, I mean without Jesus. My Guardian Angel has not left me for even a second; yet, how many omissions,[3] how many faults even in his presence! My God, have mercy on me! I always went to Communion, but Jesus was like He wasn't there anymore. But would Jesus wish to leave me alone even today on such a great holy day? I received Communion with much more consolation, but without feeling Jesus. I prayed a lot these days, because I want a grace from Jesus.

Today Mother Maria Teresa should go to Heaven; I hope so. But how will I know? I can't collect myself unless I am in a safe place.[4] Today my Guardian Angel will stand guard at my door.

Here I am at 9:15 of this great day. I feel the usual internal collection; I prayed to my Guardian Angel to stand

---

[1] 'Sins of omission', being what we should have done but did not do.
[2] Either way Gemma should be drawn closer to Jesus, which is the goal.
[3] Lack of incessant prayer (making every thought, word, and action a prayer), Bible study, contemplation on heavenly things, communion with the saints (Hebrews 12:1).
[4] People who see her as being weird or deluded pester her.

guard so that no one should see me; I hid in a room for the nuns.

Oh, not much time passed before collection was followed by rapture. (Whoever reads this should not believe anything, because I could very well be deceived; may Jesus never permit such a thing! I do so for obedience, and I oblige myself to write with great disgust.)[1]

It was around 9:30 and I was reading; all of a sudden I am shaken by a hand resting gently on my left shoulder. I turn in fright; I was afraid and tried to call, but I was held back. I turned and saw a person dressed in white; I recognized it was a woman; I looked, and her expression assured me I had nothing to fear:

'Gemma,' she said after some moments, 'do you know me?' I said no, because that was the truth; she responded:

'I am Mother Maria Teresa of the Infant Jesus: I thank you so, so much for the great concern you have shown me because soon I shall be able to attain my eternal happiness.'

All this happened while I was awake and fully aware of myself.

Then she added: 'Continue still, because I still have a few days of suffering.' And in so saying she caressed me and then went away.

Her countenance, I must say, inspired much confidence in me. From that hour I redoubled my prayers for her soul, so that soon she should reach her objective; but my prayers are too weak; how I wish that for the souls in Purgatory my prayers should have the strength of the saints.

From that moment I suffered constantly because until about 11:00 p.m. I could not be alone. I felt inside me a certain sense of collection, a desire to go and pray, but how to do it? I couldn't. How many times I had to insist! Finally I had the longed-for permission, and I went to my Mom;

---

[1] She has been commanded to keep a diary by her lifelong Father-Confessor Monsignor Volpi. She was ordered to stop writing by her new confessor and spiritual director Father Germano.

although they were only a few moments, they were precious moments!

Because of my bad behavior, Jesus did not permit the Blessed Virgin to come as she always did, smiling, but instead very sad (and I was the cause). She reproached me a little but cheered up about one thing (that I think here it would be better not to say), and this thing also gave great consolation to Jesus! And in fact it was to reward me for this thing that she came,[1] but as I said, in a serious mood; she said a few words, among them: 'Daughter, when I go to Heaven this morning, I shall take your heart with me.'[2]

In that moment I felt as if she approached— removed it from me, took it with her, in her hands, and said to me: 'Fear nothing, be good; I shall keep your heart forever up there with me, always in my hands.' She blessed me hurriedly and in going away she pronounced these words as well: 'To me you have given your heart, but Jesus wants something else as well.'

'What does he want?' I asked.

'Your will,' she answered, and vanished.[3]

I found myself on the ground, but I know exactly when that happened; it was when she began to approach me and remove my heart.

Although these things frighten me upon first appearance, still at the finish I always end up being in infinite consolations.

---

[1] i.e. Mary came to reward me about something I had done that had brought consolation to Jesus.

[2] Here we enter the realm of the spiritually fantastic and awe-inspiring, as if we haven't already been there with Gemma.

[3] The heart is the desire for godliness, the will is the practical work toward that desire. They are not the same thing, but a comparison of arduous (and sometimes deadly) Black Magic practices to get what one wants from demons (who also masquerade as so-called 'guardian angels') shows that the narrow way of Jesus is straight and easy to walk on when a little discipline is steadily applied.

Thursday, August 16

Here I am at Thursday. The usual disgust descends upon me; fear of losing my soul comes over me; the number of my sins and their enormity, all open up before me. What agitation! In these moments my Guardian Angel suggested in my ear: 'But God's mercy is infinite.' I calmed down.

Early in the day the pain in my head began; it must have been around 10:00. When I was alone, I threw myself on the bed; I suffered some, but Jesus was not long in appearing, showing me that He also suffered greatly. I reminded Him of the sinners[1] for whom He Himself urged me to offer all my little aches to the Eternal Father on their behalf.

While I was with Jesus and suffering, and He suffered also, a strong desire came upon me, almost impossible to resist. Jesus realized this, and asked me: 'What do you want me to do?'

And I immediately: 'Jesus, have pity, lighten Mother Maria Teresa's torments.'

And Jesus: 'I have already done so. Do you wish anything else?' He asked.

That gave me courage and I said: 'Jesus, save her, save her.'

And Jesus answered like this: 'On the third day after the Assumption of my Blessed Mother, she will be released from Purgatory and I will take her with me to Heaven.'

Those words filled me with a joy such that I do not know how to express it. Jesus said a number of other things; I also asked why after Holy Communion He did not allow me to taste the sweetness of Heaven. He answered promptly: 'You are not worthy, oh daughter,' but He promised that the next morning He would do it. How could

---

[1] Still on Earth and also in Purgatory, which is the 'place' of purging for Believers who did not fully apply their wills while still living.

I pass the time until morning? It's true, only a few hours remained, but for me they were years; I didn't close my eyes in sleep; I was consumed, I wanted morning to come immediately: in a word, that night seemed like forever to me, but finally morning has come.

Friday, August 17

Jesus, as soon as He arrived on my tongue (the cause so often of so many sins),[1] made Himself felt immediately. I was no longer in myself, but Jesus was in me; He descended to my breast. (I say breast because I no longer have a heart;[2] I gave it to Jesus' mom.) What happy moments I spent with Jesus! How could I return His affections? With what words could I express His love, and for this poor creature? Yet He did deign[3] to come. It's truly impossible, yes, it is impossible not to love Jesus. How many times He asked me if I love Him and if I truly love Him. And do you still doubt it, my Jesus? So, He unites ever more closely with me, talks to me, says He wants me to be perfect, that He too loves me very much and I should reciprocate.[4]

My God, how can I make myself worthy of so many graces? Where I cannot reach, my beloved Guardian Angel will take my place. May God never let me deceive myself nor others.

I spent the rest of the day united with Jesus; I suffer a little but no one sees my suffering; only from time to time

---

[1] James, in his Biblical letter, warns us about the power of a wayward tongue.

[2] The desire Gemma had since her earthly mother began to teach her when she was a young child is being kept in Heaven by Mary while Jesus still requires the disciplines, or will, which shall cause the desire (heart) to blossom into saintliness.

[3] consent

[4] Love Him in return, which completes the elliptical full circuit of *agape* or godly love.

does some lament[1] come forth but, my God, it is truly involuntary.

Today it took very little, indeed nothing, for me to collect myself: my mind was already with Jesus and I immediately went in spirit as well. How affectionate Jesus showed Himself to be today. *But how He suffers*! I do what I can to diminish the anguish, and I would do more if I had permission. He came near today, lifted the crown from my head, and then I did not see Him replace it as usual on His head; He held it in His hands, all His wounds were open, but they did not drip blood as usual. They were beautiful.

He usually blesses me before leaving, and in fact He lifted His right hand; from that hand I then *saw a ray of light shine forth, much stronger than a lamp*. He kept His hand raised; I remained fixed in watching it, I could not get enough of Him. Oh if I could make everyone know and see how beautiful is my Jesus. He blessed me with that same hand He had raised, and He left me. After this happened to me, I wanted to know the meaning of the light that shone from His wounds, in particular from His right hand, the one He blessed me with. My Guardian Angel said these words to me: 'Daughter, on this day Jesus' blessing has showered an abundance of graces upon you.'

Now that I am writing this He[2] approached me and said: 'I urge you, my daughter, always to obey, and in everything. Reveal everything to your Confessor; tell him not to neglect you but to keep you hidden.' And then He added: 'Tell him that Jesus wants him to have much more concern toward you, that he give you more thought, because otherwise you are too inexperienced.'

He repeated these things even after I had written them; He said them many times, when I was awake, and I felt as if I actually saw Him and heard Him speak. Jesus, may

---

[1] cry
[2] Jesus

your holy will always be done.

But how I suffer for the obligation to write certain things. The disgust I felt initially, instead of diminishing, keeps growing enormously, and I am enduring deathly anguish. How many times today I tried to find and burn all my writings. And then? You maybe, oh my God, You would like me to write also about those hidden things that You let me know out of your goodness in order always to keep me low and humble me? If You wish, oh Jesus, I'm ready to do even that: make Your will known. But these writings, of what benefit are they? For Your greater glory, oh Jesus, or to make me fall into more and more sin? You wished me to do so, and I did. You think about it. In the wound of Your sacred side, oh Jesus, I hide my every word.

Saturday-Sunday, August 18-19

During Holy Communion this morning Jesus let me know that tonight at midnight Mother Maria Teresa will fly to Heaven. Nothing else for now.

Jesus promised to give me a sign. Midnight has come, nothing yet; now it's 1:00 a.m., still nothing; toward 1:30 it looked to me like the Blessed Virgin would come to give me news, since the hour was approaching.

After a little while, in fact I thought I saw that Mother Teresa was coming, dressed as a Passionist, accompanied by her Guardian Angel and by Jesus. How she had changed since that day I first saw her. Laughing, she approached me and said she was truly happy and was going to enjoy her Jesus in eternity; she thanked me again and added: 'Tell Mother Giuseppa that I am happy and set her at ease.' She made a sign several times with her hand to say goodbye and together with Jesus and her Guardian Angel she flew to Heaven around 2:30 a.m. That night I suffered a lot because I too wanted to go to Heaven, but no one thought to take me.

The desire Jesus had nurtured in me for so long finally was satisfied; Mother Teresa is in Heaven; but even from Heaven she promised to return to see me.'

†

Diary Part 4

Late August 1900

Monday, August 20

Yesterday during the day I had to talk with my Guardian Angel once again; he reproached me above all for my laziness about prayer; he reminded me of many other things: all about the eyes, still, he threatened me severely. Last night in church he reminded me again of what he had said that day, telling me I would have to reckon with Jesus. Finally, before going to bed, as I was asking his blessing, he warned me that today, August 20, Jesus wished me to undergo an assault from the demon, this because for several days I had been negligent in prayer. He warned me that the devil would make every effort to prevent me from praying, especially mentally for all of today, and he would also deprive me of his visit (I mean my Guardian Angel's), but only for today.

I went to Holy Communion, but who knows in what a state! So distracted—with my mind still on last night—that is, on a bad dream, which I recognized as the work of the Devil.[1]

Oh God, the moment of the assault has come; and it was strong, even terrible I would almost say. No Sign of the

---

[1] A proper noun used as a name for the leader of the Fallen Angels, though the Bible designates him as Azazel, and when that name is not used, it is always Satan. Here 'Devil' is used as an umbrella term for evil.

Cross,[1] no scapular[2] was enough to halt the most ugly temptation one could imagine; he was so horrifying that I closed my eyes and never opened them again until I was absolutely freed.[3]

My God, if I am without sin, I owe it only to you. You be thanked. What to say in those moments? To look for Jesus and not find Him is a greater penance than the temptation itself. What I feel, only Jesus knows, who watches secretly and is pleased. At a certain point when it seemed the temptation would take on more force, it came to mind to invoke the Holy Father of Jesus, and I shouted: 'Eternal Father, for the Blood of Jesus free me.'

I don't know what happened; that good-for-nothing devil gave me such a strong shove that I fell off the bed, causing me to bang my head on the floor with such great force that I felt a sharp pain; I fainted and remained on the ground for a long time before regaining consciousness.

Jesus be thanked, that today also everything turned out in the best way, as He wished. The rest of the day went wonderfully. In the evening, as it happens to me many times, all my grave sins came to mind, but with such enormity that I had to make a great effort not to cry out loud: I felt a pain more alive than I had ever undergone before. The number of my sins surpasses by a thousand fold my age and my capacity; but what consoled me is that I endured the greatest pain because of my sins, so that I

---

[1] The thumb, forefinger, and middle finger are held together to represent the Trinity, the remaining two fingers representing the Humanity and Godhood of Jesus. Then, in Roman Catholicism the forehead (crown of thorns), abdomen (feet), left then right shoulders (left and right hands) are touched before the whole hand then rests on the breast (the wound in Jesus' side from which flow Blood and Water as we are reborn from above).

[2] Two pieces of cloth joined by shoulder bands and worn under clothing on the chest and back as a sacramental.

[3] Reading the writings of Gemma closely, we can see that one of the most powerful temptations she endured was unchastity.

wished this pain would never be canceled from my mind and never be diminished. My God! to what point my malice has reached!

This evening, to say the truth, I was awaiting Jesus—no way! No one showed up; only my Guardian Angel does not cease to watch over me, to instruct me, and to give me wise counsel. Many times during the day he reveals himself to me and talks to me. Yesterday he kept me company while I ate, but he didn't force me like the others do. After I had eaten, I didn't feel at all well, so he brought me a cup of coffee so good that I was healed instantly, and then he made me rest a little. Many times I make him ask Jesus for permission to stay with me all night; he goes to ask and then he does not leave me until morning, if Jesus approves.

Tuesday, August 21

I may perhaps be wrong, but today I await a little visit from Brother Gabriel, and if this is true, I have a lot to talk about with him. Jesus, give light, give light not to me but to Father Germano and to my Confessor.

Wednesday, August 22

Yesterday my Guardian Angel informed me that in the course of the day Jesus would come; he[1] yelled at me, called me conceited, but then we made up quickly. I did not think further about Jesus' visit because I did not believe it; but in getting ready for evening prayers I felt in union with Jesus, who instantly reproached me sweetly, saying: 'Gemma, don't you want me any more?'

'Oh my God, my God,' I answered him. 'What do you mean, I don't seek you? I desire you everywhere, I want

---

[1] her Guardian Angel, not Jesus

40

you, I seek you always, I yearn only for you.'[1]

Then right away it came to my mind to ask him: 'But Jesus, you came tonight, so that means You won't come tomorrow night?' He promised me that He would. But my Confessor told me that my conscience would be responsible if I suffered and then did not feel well; if I feel well, I may suffer the usual hour with Jesus; if not, let Jesus come anyway but without making me suffer; I may stay with Him and have compassion for Him and take part with Him in the deathly sadness He suffered in the Garden of Olives. Anyway, I shall obey.

Jesus also spoke to me, without my bringing it up, of the holy soul of Mrs. Giuseppina Imperiali.[2] 'Oh how dear she is to Me!' Jesus repeated. 'See,' He added, 'how much she suffers, without a moment of peace. Happiness to her!' He left me with an ineffable sense of consolation, as usual.

For the grace of Jesus and for His infinite mercy, my Guardian Angel does not leave me for even a tiny second. Yesterday I saw several angels: mine assisted me continuously and I saw another for another person, and here there certainly is no need to record further all the details; if obedience should require it, I shall be ready, but for now— that is enough—If necessary, I shall remember.

Thursday, August 23

Alas, evening comes and the usual coldness, the usual repugnance assails me; fatigue would want to win over me, but with a little effort I never want to neglect to do my duty.

Tonight Jesus placed His crown on my head at about 10:00, after I had been collected for a little while. My

---

[1] Here her desire is strong, but she still has great difficulty with her will—which is what Jesus wants from her.

[2] A friend who confides to Gemma all her preoccupations about her family and the future life of her sons.

suffering, which in no way equals Jesus', was very strong: even all my teeth hurt; any movement brought a sharp pain; I thought I could not resist, but instead I did, everything went well.

I offered those little penances for sinners and in particular for my poor soul. I begged Him to return soon. When He was about to leave, a contest sprang up between me and Jesus: which of us would be the first to visit (and I went first, I mean to Holy Communion) and together we said and we agreed that I would go to Him and He would come to me. He promised me the assistance of my holy Angel, and He left me.

Friday, August 24

Later Jesus returned to take back His crown, but He came very early, saying I had already done a lot; and since I did not want to, because I did not keep it the usual number of hours, He answered that I was still little, and this is more than enough. I suffered continuously for several hours; Jesus caressed me a lot. At a certain point in our discussion I asked enlightenment for my Confessor; on that point my Guardian Angel had tattled on Jesus. The morning before, he[1] had told me how Father Germano[2] is enlightened about me and how he cares for me. I mentioned this to Jesus without thinking, and Jesus did not know that my Guardian Angel had told me this; He made a serious face and told me He did not want my Guardian Angel to tattle on Him.[3]

---

[1] the angel

[2] Her near-future spiritual guide who has her stop writing her diary.

[3] Is Jesus really mad at the angel? Highly unlikely. Does He really not know what the angel says and does? Impossible, since Jesus is God. Then why feign anger? Gemma explains the result: more intimacy was developed—co-creation—so that she even felt comfortable enough to ask if Jesus might not do something, and we can assume she meant punish her Guardian Angel for his loose tongue. The whole episode has all been for Gemma's benefit.

While He was talking in this way, instead of being speechless, as happens when Jesus becomes serious or severe, I was taken, on the contrary, with more intimacy toward Him, and I asked: 'Jesus, could you not—' I kept quiet, thinking to make myself understood without speaking further, and Jesus did understand instantly and responded: 'Do not be afflicted, my daughter: we will make use of Father Germano soon enough. Do you understand?' He asked.

'Yes,' I answered.

And at the end he repeated these words: 'Fear not, because soon we will use him.' He raised His hand goodbye and disappeared.

Still later, I went to church for the usual blessing, but I felt tired; in fact, I truly was, but it is not, as I've said many times, true tiredness; it is laziness, a lack of desire to pray. My Guardian Angel whispered in my ear that I should pray even while sitting. At first I could not give in, but he insisted a second time, and so for obedience I remained sitting. For sure I was pleased about this, since I was unable to stay on my knees.

Last night he also made me understand that when Jesus complains[1] about me because I do not do my meditation, He does not mean Thursday and Friday, He means the other days of the week; in fact it's true, because on those two days I never forget. I promised to be more conscientious, and he ordered me to bed, saying I was tired and I had to sleep. I urged him to stay with me, but he made no promise, and in fact he did not stay.

'Now then,' I said to him, 'run to Jesus and plead with him, because tomorrow evening I must go to confession and I need to see Him'; and he instantly responded: 'And if Brother Gabriel should come?'

---

[1] As much as a righteous earthly king would complain to his cupbearer about a royal shepherd, vinedresser, or farmer. Not a complaint at all, but meant to be conveyed to the servant for his benefit.

43

'That would be the same,' I answered. 'Either Jesus or Brother Gabriel, one way or another I need a visit; beg Him to concede me this grace, I need it.'

'Can you tell me?' he asked.

'As for you,' I responded, 'go to Jesus and tell him everything and then return and tell me.' He nodded yes.

He had spoken to me a few minutes ago about Brother Gabriel and, as always, even just hearing about him made me happy all over, so I could not refrain from exclaiming: 'Brother Gabriel, how long I have been awaiting him, how much I desire him!'

'Just so, because you have such a strong desire, Jesus does not want to satisfy you.' Then, laughing, he instructed me that when Jesus came I should not let him know that I had a desire to see Brother Gabriel, in which case Jesus would grant my wish easily.

I realized he was kidding, because I know nothing can be hidden from Jesus.[1]

'Show indifference,' he repeated, 'and you will see that Jesus will send him more often.'[2]

'I won't be able to do that,' I said.

'I'll teach you; you have to talk like this to Jesus: If he comes, fine, if not, it's all the same.' And in saying this he laughed heartily.

So I also repeated the phrase but I understood that he was having fun. He ordered me to bed, saying I had to stay alone that night, because if he stayed I would never get to sleep, and he left. It's true, because when he is there I do not sleep: he teaches me so many things about Heaven and the night passes quickly, very quickly. But last night was not like that: he left me alone, and I slept, although I did awaken several times, and instantly he said: 'Sleep, otherwise I'm going away for real.'

---

[1] This is a key understanding.

[2] God hates our desires when they are inordinate and thus selfish, even if we believe them to be spiritually based and for our benefit.

44

I heard loud thunderclaps, very loud, and I was afraid; so he came and made himself visible; he blessed me once again and I went back to sleep.

Saturday, August 25

During Communion this morning no consolation; I did everything coldly. Let the holy will of my God be done. What will happen today? Jesus is not coming, and I don't even feel Him nearby. I go to bed and I see a Guardian Angel approaching, whom I recognized to be mine; but I was overtaken with a bit of fear and an internal disquiet.

So many times fear assails me when I see someone appear, but little by little this passes and ends in consolation. Yesterday, instead, my disquiet grew until, if someone touched me, I shook: something that never happens to me when it is truly my dear angel. In short, I was uncertain about this when he asked me: 'When are you going to confession?'

'This evening,' I answered.

'And why? Why do you go so often? Don't you know that your Confessor is a swindler?' Then I understood what was happening here[1] and I made the Sign of the Cross several times; he struck me so severely that I shook. My angel never speaks to me this way.

The combat lasted in this way for a long while, and I promised that in spite of him I would go to confession, and in fact I went. I called Jesus, and my Mom,[2] but what! No one. After a while my real Guardian Angel appeared, obliging me to confess every detail, and he specified two things to tell my Confessor.

Distress and fear of the enemy vanished quickly, and I calmed down until it was time to go to confession; I didn't

---

[1] A demon masquerading as her Guardian Angel, and being convincing about the disguise until its words reveal its true nature.
[2] Mary

want to go for anything. With effort I went, but I was able to say very, very little. But I do want to tell everything, so I will write.

Last night my beloved Mother came, but her visit was so short; nevertheless it consoled me greatly. I prayed to her as much as I could on my own behalf, that she take me to Heaven, and I also prayed fervidly for other matters. How she smiled when I repeatedly called her Mom! She came near, caressed me, and left me in the company of my Guardian Angel, who remained joyful and cheerful until morning.

Sunday, August 26

In the morning, after I left my room, he also left. I received Holy Communion without knowing anything of Jesus;[1] during the morning I felt such a strong wish to cry that I had to hide myself out of the sight of others so they wouldn't notice. My soul felt uneasy and I did not know what to rely on. My God, how shall I begin to describe it! But it's for the best, because if this notebook of mine should fall into people's hands, they will recognize in me nothing other than a disobedient, bad person.[2]

Yesterday, while eating, I raised my eyes and saw my Guardian Angel looking at me with an expression so severe I was frightened; he did not speak. Later, when I went to bed for a moment, my God! he commanded me to look him in the face; I looked and then almost immediately I lowered my gaze, but he insisted and said: 'Aren't you ashamed to commit sins in my presence? You certainly feel ashamed after you commit them!' He insisted I look at him; for more than half an hour he made me stay in his presence looking

---

[1] She felt nothing in the moments when Jesus should be most present with us, since His command is that we never forget Him.

[2] By God's will, it did fall into the hands of others, and has been studied for over a hundred years to date (2018).

him in the face; he gave me some very stern looks.

I did nothing but cry. I commended myself to my God, to our Mother, to get me out of there, because I could not resist much longer. Every so often he repeated: 'I am ashamed of you.' I prayed that others would not see him in that state, because then no one would ever come near me; I don't know if others saw him.

I suffered for an entire day, and whenever I lifted my eyes, he always looked at me sternly; I could not collect myself for even a minute. That evening I said my prayers anyway, and he was always there watching me with the same expression; he let me go to bed, but he did bless me; he never abandoned me: he stayed with me for several hours, without speaking and always stern. I never did have the courage to speak a word to him; I only said: 'My God, what shame if others should see my angel so angry!'

There was no way I could sleep last night; I was awake until after 2:00; I know, because I heard the clock strike. I stayed in bed, not moving, my mind turned to God but without praying.[1] Finally, after the clock struck 3:00, I saw my Guardian Angel approaching; he placed his hand on my forehead and said these words: 'Sleep, bad girl.' I saw him no more.

Monday, August 27

This morning I received Holy Communion: I hardly had the courage to receive it. Jesus seemed to let me know a little about why my Guardian Angel was acting this way: I had made my last confession badly. Unfortunately, this was true.

---

[1] Here we see that either Gemma doesn't fully understand what praying is, being always in a constant state of meditation on the things of God—or she is speaking of specifically asking for guidance for herself or others.

Tuesday, August 28

My Guardian Angel remained very stern until this morning, after I revealed everything to my Confessor.[1] Upon my exiting from the confessional, he looked at me happily, with an air of kindness: I returned from death to life. Later he spoke to me on his own (I did not have the courage to question him) he asked me how I was, because I was not feeling well the night before. I answered that only he could cure me; he came near, caressed me again and again, and said I should be good.

Repeatedly I asked him if he loved me as much as before and if he loved me despite everything; he answered in this way: 'Today I am not ashamed of you, yesterday I was.' I asked many times for forgiveness and he indicated that I was forgiven for every past action. Finally, I sent him to Jesus for three things: (1) If He was happy with me now? (2) If He had forgiven everything? (3) That He should rid me of this shame so that I could be obedient to my Confessor.

He went away instantly and returned very late; he said Jesus was very happy; that He has forgiven me, but for the last time;[2] as to the shame, he said Jesus responded with these exact words: 'Tell her to obey perfectly.' Later, then, I went to bed, and after a little while I felt some remorse. I was thinking, it's true, on the subject of a meditation on the Passion, but in bed. My Guardian Angel asked what I was thinking. 'About the Passion,' I answered. 'What will Jesus say about me, who leads such an easy life, praying little, and in bed; in short, all my time in prayer I spend in bed?' Unfortunately, all this is true. He answered by asking what I thought. 'It is laziness,' I responded. But I promised that from that evening on I would never again pray in bed;

---

[1] Monsignor Volpi

[2] This seems harsh until we grasp fully that Jesus never wants any of us to enter Purgatory. He would rather we do all of the work while living.

except for the day that I was supposed to, out of obedience. Last evening and for the whole night he never left me, but with an agreement: I must be quiet and sleep. I did it.

Wednesday, August 29

Today there's one thing I shall do: I want to write a little note to Brother Gabriel; then I'll give it to my Guardian Angel and await a reply. And we're going to do this without Jesus knowing; he himself said we will not tell Jesus anything.[1]

And I did it: I wrote a very long letter; I spoke of all my experiences without leaving out anything; then I advised my Guardian Angel that it was ready, and if he wanted to— This evening, Wednesday, I placed it under my pillow, and this morning when I got up I didn't think about checking because I had better things in mind: I was going to Jesus.[2]

Thursday, August 30

As soon as I returned, I looked, and how odd! The letter wasn't there anymore. I say odd because I heard from others that this is a strange happening; but to me it doesn't seem so. My Guardian Angel then asked me if I needed an answer. I laughed. 'What else,' I told him. 'Of course I need one.'

'All right,' he said, 'but until Saturday you can't have one.'

Patience, until Saturday then.

In the meantime, here I am at Thursday evening. Oh God! All my sins are paraded before me. What an

---

[1] Gemma knows that nothing can be hidden from Jesus, as she says a bit earlier, but, as with most of us, Reality is sometimes too large for her to fully grasp, as in this case when she is trying to write a note to the saint Gabriel Possenti without Jesus knowing about it.
[2] Mass and Holy Communion

enormity! Yes, all of you should know; my life until now has been a continuous series of sins. Always I see their great quantity, and the malicious intent with which I committed them, especially when Thursday evening approaches; they parade before me in a manner so frightening that I become ashamed and unbearable even to myself. So, especially that evening, I make resolutions and repent continuously; but then I keep none of them and return to my usual ways. A little strength, a little courage comes to me when I feel Jesus at the hour when he places the crown of thorns on me and makes me suffer until Friday evening, because this I offer for sinful souls, especially my own.

This is how things went yesterday evening, Thursday; I thought Jesus would do like usual that evening: He placed the crown of thorns on my head, the cause of so much pain for my beloved Jesus, and left it there for several hours. It made me suffer a little, but when I say suffering I mean taking pleasure. It is a pleasure, that suffering. How He was afflicted! And the cause: for the many sins committed, and the many ungrateful souls whom He assists, only to receive in return exactly the opposite. Of this ingratitude how much I feel guilty myself! For sure, Jesus must have spoken of me.

My Guardian Angel warned me that the hour allowed to me for obedience had ended; what to do? Jesus would have stayed longer, but He saw clearly the embarrassing situation I found myself in. I reminded myself about obedience, and for obedience I should have sent Jesus away, because the hour was up.

'Come on,' said Jesus. 'Give me a sign now that you will always obey.'

So I exclaimed: 'Jesus, you can go away because now I don't want you anymore.'[1] And Jesus smiled as He blessed

---

[1] Gemma is obviously joking with our King when she says this.

me, along with all the members of the *Sacro Collegio*, and He commended me to my Guardian Angel,[1] and left me so happy that I cannot express myself.

As usual, that night I cannot sleep because I am united with Jesus, united more closely than usual, and also because I think my head aches a bit; I kept vigil together with my beloved Angel.

Friday, August 31

In the morning I ran to receive Holy Communion, but I could not say anything; I just stayed in silence; the pain in my head impeded me. My God, how much I lack in this! Jesus held back nothing on my behalf while I instead, in order not to suffer, avoid making even the slightest movement if I can. What would you say, my Jesus, about this laziness and ill will?

All morning I did nothing but rest. Day came, and effortlessly I flew to Jesus; He lifted the thorns and asked if I had suffered much.

'Oh, my Jesus,' I exclaimed, 'the suffering begins now because You go away. Yesterday and today, I took much pleasure because I felt close to You; but from now on, until You return, it will truly be constant suffering for me.' I implored Him. 'Come, my Jesus, come more often: I will be good, I will always obey everyone. Make me happy, Jesus.' I suffered as I spoke this way because, little by little, Jesus was leaving me.

Finally after a short while He left me alone, once again in the usual state of abandonment. Toward evening I went to confession and the Confessor, believing I was not feeling well, because I had been suffering some, ordered me to go to bed as soon as I entered my room, and he ordered me to

---

[1] 'commended… Guardian Angel = 'Jesus left my Guardian Angel in charge of me'

sleep, without speaking with my Guardian Angel (because sometimes we would talk for hours on end), and that I should sleep.

I went to bed but I could not fall asleep out of the curiosity I had; I wanted to ask my Guardian Angel so many things, and I waited for him to speak on his own, but no way! All he told me was to go to sleep, several times. Finally I fell asleep.

Saturday, September 1

This morning on his own he awakened me early and said that today I would have an answer. 'How?' I asked.

'You will see,' he said, laughing.

For all of today I stayed without any temptations; toward evening one suddenly came over me, in the ugliest manner. But here I don't think it would be good to tell, because it's too—

Who would have imagined that my beloved Mother would come to see me? I wasn't even thinking about it because I believed my bad conduct wouldn't allow it; but she took pity on me, and in a short time I felt collected; following this collection, as so often happened, my head took off. I found myself (I thought) with Our Lady of Sorrows. What happiness in those moments. How dear to pronounce the name Mom! What sweetness I felt in my heart in those moments! Let whoever is able to, explain it. It seemed to me, after a few minutes of commotion, that she took me in her lap and made me rest my head on her shoulder, keeping me there a while. My heart in that moment was filled with happiness and contentment; I could desire nothing more.

'Do you love no one but me?' she asked from time to time.

'Oh no,' I answered. 'I love someone else even more than you.'

'And who is that?' she asked, pretending not to know.

'It's a person who is most dear to me, more than anything else; I love Him so much I would give up my life this very instant; because of Him I no longer care about my body.'

'But tell me who He is,' she asked impatiently. 'If you had come the evening before last, you would have seen Him staying with me. But you see, He comes to me very rarely, while I go to Him every day, and I would go even more often if I could. But do you know, dear Mother,' I said, 'why He does this? Because He wants to see whether at so great a distance I might become capable of not loving Him anymore; instead, the further away He is, the more I feel drawn to him.'

She repeated: 'Tell me who He is.'

'No, I won't tell you,' I responded. 'You should see, dear Mom, how His beauty resembles yours, your hair is the same color as His.'

And it seemed my Mom was caressing me as she said, 'But, my daughter, who are you talking about?'

And I exclaimed loudly: 'Don't you understand me? I'm talking about Jesus. *About Jesus*,' I repeated even more loudly.

She looked at me, smiling, and she hugged me tightly to her: 'Go ahead and love Him, love Him very much, *but love only Him*.'[1]

'Don't be afraid,' I said. 'No one in the world shall taste my affections, only Jesus.'

She hugged me again, and it seemed like She kissed me on the forehead; I awoke and found myself on the floor, with the crucifix nearby.

---

[1] Every Christian needs to hear these words and take them fully to heart.

Whoever reads these things, I repeat again, should not believe, because they are all my imagination; nevertheless I agree to describe everything, because I am bound by obedience, otherwise I would do differently. I believed that from day to day the repugnance I experience in writing certain things would finally cease, but instead it always increases: it is a punishment such that I cannot withstand, I almost die from it.

Sunday, September 2

Tonight I slept with my Guardian Angel by my side; upon awakening I saw him next to me; he asked me where I was going. 'To Jesus,' I answered.

The rest of the day went very well. But my God, toward evening what happened! My Guardian Angel got serious and stern; I could not figure out the reason, but he, from whom nothing can be hidden, in a stern tone (at the moment when I started to recite my usual prayers) asked me what I was doing.

'I am praying.'

'Who are you waiting for?' (becoming yet more serious).

Without thinking, I said: 'Brother Gabriel.'

Upon hearing me pronounce those words he started to yell at me, saying I was waiting in vain, just as I could wait in vain for the response [to my letter] because—

And here I remember two sins I had committed during the day. My God, what sternness! He pronounced these words more than once: 'I am ashamed of you. I will end up by not coming to you anymore, and maybe—who knows if even tomorrow.' And he left me in that state. He made me cry so much. I want to ask forgiveness but when he is that angry, there is no way he wants to forgive.

Monday, September 3

I did not see him again that night, nor this morning; today
he told me to adore Jesus, who was alone, and then he
disappeared again.

This evening it was much better than the evening before;
I asked him many times for forgiveness and he seemed
willing to forgive me. Tonight he stayed with me
constantly: he repeated that I should be good and not give
further disgust to our Jesus, and when I am in his presence,
I should try to be better.

Translator's Preface
to the
Autobiography of
Gemma Galgani

Many years ago, when I was a young priest, I had the good fortune of studying for a time in Rome. During that time, I lived with the Passionist Community at their central house in Rome, Sts. John and Paul. This was an international community of Passionists, but largely Italian, and the language of the house was Italian. As a result, I ended my stay in Rome with at least some knowledge of the Italian language.

I returned to the States with many memories, and with a desire to put my acquired knowledge of Italian to some practical use. Among many other Roman experiences, I had come into more direct contact with the person and the writings of St. Gemma Galgani. Gemma was a young lay woman who desired ardently to become a Passionist nun, but God never granted this desire. However, through her close association with the Passionists, she earned a treasured place among the Passionist Family. As so many others have done through the years, I found that I had fallen under the spell of St. Gemma. And so, when it came to a way of putting my knowledge of Italian to use, I naturally thought of doing something with the writings of St. Gemma, which, until that time remained locked in the Italian, at least as far as English readers were concerned.

It may be a cause of surprise for many, even now, to learn that this humble and hidden saint wrote a great deal. There are two large volumes of her writings published in Italian. One volume, *Lettere di S. Gemma Galgani* contains 459 pages of her letters alone. Another, *Estasi-Diario-Autobiografia-Scritti Vari di S. Gemma Galgani* contains

316 pages of her other writings. One does not have to read far in either of these volumes to be completely captivated by the simple and humble saint.

Gemma wrote her autobiography at the insistent request of Father Germanus, C. P., who became her spiritual director in January 1900, approximately three years before her death. At first he directed his spiritual daughter by letter, coming to Lucca to see her for the first time in September 1900. He found Gemma writing a diary of the graces she received day by day. She was writing this diary under obedience to her regular Confessor, Msgr. Volpi, Auxiliary Bishop of Lucca. Judging on general principles that it was not good to concentrate to such an extent on what was happening within, Father Germanus ordered her to stop and made her hand over to him all that she had written. But later, as he read the diary, he realized that while the principle on which he had acted was true, it did not apply to Gemma's case. He realized, in short, that he was dealing with a most extraordinary person.

In order to remedy this mistake, he asked her to write for him a general confession of all her sins that he might be better able to direct her. He knew that she could not write of her sins without telling the graces which made them appear so great to her. Gemma complied with his wish, though with great reluctance as is indicated by the autobiography itself.

In her letters, Gemma always refers to this document as her general confession. At the same time, however, it is evident that she did not look upon it as a sacramental confession. At least twice in the pages of the autobiography she passes over points, explaining that she will tell him in confession.

The autobiography thus written in obedience to Father Germanus filled 93 pages of a notebook, all written in her own hand. It covers the years from her infancy until September 1900, when she was 22 years old. She began writing the autobiography on February 17, 1901, and finished it in May of the same year. Since she died two years later on April 11, 1903, it does not cover the last two years of her life.

The manuscript copy of the autobiography still exists and is on display at Sts. John and Paul in Rome. Gemma's beautiful handwriting is still plain, but a remarkable fact about the notebook is that every page has the appearance of having been burned. Father Germanus explains this phenomenon in his life of St. Gemma:

'Gemma's manuscript, when finished, was by my orders given to the charge of her adopted mother, Signora Cecilia Giannini, who kept it hidden in a drawer awaiting the first opportunity of handing it to me. Some days elapsed and Gemma thought she saw the demon pass through the window of the room where the drawer was, chuckling, and then disappearing in the air. Accustomed as she was to such apparitions, she thought nothing of it. But he, having returned shortly after to molest her, as often happened, with a repulsive temptation, and having failed, left gnashing his teeth and declaring exultantly: 'War, war, your book is in my hands.' So she wrote to tell me. Then, owing to the obedience which she was under to disclose to her vigilant benefactress everything extraordinary that happened to her, she thought she was obliged to tell her what had occurred. They went, opened the drawer, and found that the book was no longer there. I was written to at once and it was easy to imagine my consternation at having lost such a treasure. What was to be done? I thought a great deal about it, and just then, while at the tomb of Blessed Gabriel of the Dolors, a fresh idea came to my mind. I resolved to exorcise the devil and thus force him to return the manuscript if he had really taken it. With my ritual stole and holy water I went to the tomb of the blessed servant of God and there, although nearly four hundred

58

miles from Lucca, I pronounced the exorcism in regular form. God seconded my ministry, and at the same hour the writing was restored to the place from which it had been taken several days before. But in what a state! The pages from top to bottom were all smoked, and parts burned, as if each one had been separately exposed over a strong fire. Yet they were not so badly burned as to destroy the writing. This document, having thus passed through a hell fire, is in my hands.'

Having seen the Autobiography as it is preserved today, I can witness personally the evidence described by Father Germanus. We leave it to the reader to judge why the devil was so jealous of this document.

My translation of the Autobiography was published in two places at the time: 'The Passionist', July 1954; and 'Cross and Crown', June and September 1955. It gives me much pleasure that the *Autobiography of St. Gemma* is being republished in its present form.

One final note, in both of the above publications the name Columban Browning, C. P. was given as the translator. Sometime after that, I returned to my baptismal name.

Rev. William Browning, C.P.

†

The Autobiography
of
Gemma Galgani

To my dear Father, who will burn it immediately.

My dear Father,[1]

You must understand that at first I intended to make a general confession of my sins without adding anything else, but your Guardian Angel reproved me, and told me to obey and give a short summary of all that has happened in my life, both good and bad.

How difficult it is, dear Father, to obey in this matter! But please be careful. You may read and reread this as often as you wish but do not show it to anyone else, and when you are through with it burn it up immediately. Do you understand?

The angel promised to help me recall everything to mind. I told him plainly and pleaded with him that I do not want to do this. I was frightened at the thought of recalling everything, but the angel assured me that he would help me.

I think, dear Father, that when you read this and learn of all my sins you will be angry with me and will no longer want to be my Father. Still I hope that you will always be willing— So prepare yourself to learn of every kind of sin.

And you, dear Father, do you approve of what the angel told me, that I should speak of my whole life? That's his order and I take for granted that's what is in your mind and heart. By writing everything, both good and bad, you will

---

[1] Germanus, her new spiritual director and confessor after Fr. Volpi.

be able to see better how bad I have been and how good others have been to me. You will see how ungrateful I have shown myself toward Jesus and how much I have failed to listen to the good advice of my parents and teachers.

So I begin the task, dear Father. Live Jesus!

†

The first thing I remember is that when I was a little girl not seven years old, my mother used to take me into her arms, and often when she did this she cried and said to me: 'I have prayed so much that Jesus would give me a little girl. He has given me this consolation; it is true, but too late. I am ill,' she would say to me, 'and I must die. I must leave you. Oh, if I could only take you with me! Would you come?'

I understood very little of this, but I wept because I saw my mother weeping. 'And where are you going?' I asked her.

'To Heaven with Jesus and the angels,' she replied.

It was my mother, dear Father,[1] who first made me want to go to Heaven when I was just a little child. And when I still show this desire, I am reprimanded and receive an emphatic 'No' for an answer.

But when my mother asked me this I told her that I did want to go with her. And I remember that when she spoke so often of taking me to Heaven with her I did not want to be separated from her. I would not even leave her room.

The doctor forbade me to go near mother's bed, but such a command was useless, for I did not obey. Every evening before going to bed I would go to her and, kneeling beside her bed, I would say my prayers.

One evening she had me add to the usual prayers a *De*

---

[1] She addresses her new spiritual advisor Father Germano of St. Stanislaus, who has requested this autobiography from her.

Profundis[1] to the souls in Purgatory and five Gloria's[2] to the Wounds of Jesus. I said these prayers, but as usual carelessly and without attention (all my life I have never paid attention to my prayers).[3] I made a great show over it, complaining to my mother that these were too many prayers to say and I didn't want to say them. And she, indulgent as she was, shortened the prayers after that.[4]

Meanwhile, the time was coming when I was to receive Confirmation.[5] I wanted to take some instructions because I knew nothing. But, bad as I was, I would not leave my mother's room and a catechist[6] had to come to our house

---

[1] *Out of the depths I cry to You, O Lord; Lord, hear my voice.*
Let Your ears be attentive to my voice in supplication.
If You, O Lord, mark iniquities, Lord, who can stand?
But with You is forgiveness, that You may be revered.
I trust in the Lord; my soul trusts in His word.
My soul waits for the Lord more than sentinels wait for the dawn.
More than sentinels wait for the dawn, let Israel wait for the Lord,
For with the Lord is kindness and with Him is plenteous redemption;
And He will redeem Israel from all their iniquities.

[2] *Glory to God in the highest. And on earth peace to men of good will. We praise You. We bless You. We adore you. We glorify You. We give You thanks for Your great glory. O Lord God, heavenly King, God the Father almighty. O Lord Jesus Christ, the Only-begotten Son. O Lord God, Lamb of God, Son of the Father: you Who take away the sins of the world, have mercy on us. You Who take away the sins of the world, receive our prayer. You Who sit at the right hand of the Father, have mercy on us. For you alone are holy. You alone are the Lord. You alone, O Jesus Christ, are most high. Together with the Holy Spirit in the glory of God the Father.*

[3] Here we see Gemma confess that her desire has been strong but that her will has not been. The old, wise saying can be applied: 'Good intentions pave the road to Hell.' Desire commands that sainthood be accomplished, but the will must serve the desire to see that the job is accomplished.

[4] Meaning well, her mother wounded her spiritually.

[5] The sealing of Christian devotion begun at baptism.

[6] A teacher of the basic tenets of Christian belief.

every evening where I took the instructions in the presence of my mother.

On the 26th of May, 1885, I received Confirmation, but I did so weeping. For after the function there was to be a Mass, and I was always afraid that Mother would go away without taking me with her.

I assisted at the Mass as best I could, all the while praying for her. All of a sudden I heard a voice in my heart saying to me: 'Are you willing to give your mother to me?'

'Yes,' I answered, 'if you will take me, too.'

'No,' replied the voice. 'Give me your mother willingly. But you must remain with your father for the present. I will take your mother to Heaven, understand? Do you give her to me willingly?'

I was forced to give my consent. When the Mass was over I ran home. Oh, my God! I looked at Mother and wept. I simply could not contain myself.

Two more months passed. I never left her side. But finally my father, who feared that I would die before Mother, forced me to leave one day and took me to the home of my mother's brother who lived near Lucca.

Father, dear Father,[1] such was my lot. What a torture it was! I did not see anyone, neither my father nor my brothers. I learned that my mother died on September 17 of that year.

My life was changed when I went to live with my uncle. My aunt was there but she was in no way like my mother. She was good and religious but was interested in the Church only to a certain point. I had formerly complained that my mother had made me pray too much. But all the time that I was with my aunt I could not even go to confession (which I wanted so much). I had been to confession only seven times and I wanted to go every day after the death of my mother (my mother had made me go

---

[1] Again she addresses Germano.

every week after my confirmation).

My aunt decided to keep me as her daughter, but my brother, who is now dead, learned of it and would not allow it. So, on Christmas Day I returned to my family and lived with my father, my brothers, my two sisters (one of whom I did not know because she had been taken away shortly after her birth), and two servants.

What consolation I experienced on returning to my family and being out of the hands of my aunt! She wanted the best for me, but I wanted none of it. My father then sent me to school at the Institute of St. Zita, which was conducted by nuns.

During the time when I was with my aunt, I was always bad. She had a son who was always tormenting me, pulling my hands behind me. One day when he was on a horse (15 hands high) my aunt told me to take him some kind of a coat to put on. I took it to him, and when I was near, he pinched me. Then I gave him a hard push, and he fell off and hurt his head. In punishment, my aunt tied my hands behind me for the entire day. Thus mistreated, I got very angry and I told him so with strong words. I even threatened to get even, but did not do so.

I started to school at the nuns' school and it was Heaven for me. I immediately expressed my desire to make my first Communion, but they found me so bad and so ignorant that they discouraged me from it. They began, however, to instruct me and to give me much good advice. But I only became worse. Nevertheless, my only desire was to make my first Communion soon and they, knowing how strong was my desire, granted my request before long.

The nuns used to have the children make their first Communion in the month of June. The time had come and I had to ask my father's permission to enter the convent for a short time. My father, who was indisposed, did not grant me permission. But I knew a very clever way to make him let me do anything, so I used it and got the permission at once. (Every time my father saw me weeping, he would grant me whatever I wanted.) I cried, otherwise I would not have received the permission. In the evening he gave it, and early the next morning I went into the convent where I remained for fifteen days. During this time I saw none of my family. But how happy I was! What a Heaven it was, dear Father!

Once inside the convent, I found it to my liking, and ran to the chapel to thank Jesus. I begged him fervently to prepare me for Holy Communion.

But I had also another desire besides this. When I was a little girl, my mother used to show me the crucifix and tell me that Christ died on the cross for men. Later on, my teachers taught me the same thing, but I had never understood it. Now I wanted to know all about the life and Passion of Jesus. I told my teacher of this desire, and she began, day by day, to explain these things to me, choosing for this a time when the other children were in bed. She did this, I believe, without the Mother Superior knowing of it.

One evening when she was explaining something to me about the Crucifixion, the crowning with thorns, and all the sufferings of Jesus, she explained it so very well that a great sorrow and compassion came over me. So much so that I was seized immediately with fever so intense that I was forced to remain in bed all the next day. From that day on, the teacher explained such things only briefly.

These nuns caused me some disquiet. They wanted to inform my father that I had contracted the fever. But it did cause a lot of trouble, not only for me but for them and for the whole convent. This happened especially during the ten days of the retreat.

With eleven other children I began the retreat on the 9th day of June. Father Raphael Cianetti preached the retreat. All the children devoted themselves eagerly to prepare well to receive Jesus. Among so many, only I was very negligent and distracted. I gave no thought to changing my life. I listened to the sermons but very soon forgot what I heard.[1]

Often, even every day, that good Father said: 'He who eats of Jesus will live of His life.' These words filled me with much consolation, and I reasoned with myself: *Therefore when Jesus comes to me I will no longer live of myself because Jesus will live in me.* And I nearly died of the desire to be able to say these words soon ('Jesus lives in me'). Sometimes I would spend whole nights meditating on these words, being consumed with desire.

Finally the day I wanted so much arrived. The day before I wrote these few lines to my father:

Dear Papa,

Today is the vigil of my first Holy Communion, a day of great joy for me. I write these lines to assure you of my affection and to beg you to pray to Jesus that the first time He comes to me He may find me disposed to receive all those graces that He has prepared for me.

I beg your pardon for all the displeasures and all the disobedience that I have been guilty of, and I beg you this evening to forget all these things. Asking your blessing, I am

Your affectionate daughter,

Gemma

†

---

[1] Her desire is strong, but her will is almost nonexistent. The fantasy of being a spiritual person attracted her, but the required work was odious to her.

I prepared myself, with much work on the part of those good nuns, for my general confession. I made it in three sessions to Msgr. Volpi. I finished it on Saturday, the vigil of that happy day.

Finally, Sunday morning came. I arose early and ran to Jesus for the first time. At last my desires were realized. I understood for the first time the promise of Jesus: 'He who eats of Me shall live of My life.'

Dear Father, I do not know how to tell what passed between Jesus and me at that moment. Jesus made Himself felt very strongly by my poor soul. I understood at that moment that the delights of Heaven are not like those of the Earth. I felt myself overcome by the desire to render that union with my God continual. I felt weary of the world more and more, and more disposed to recollection.[1] It was that same morning that Jesus gave me the great desire to be a religious.[2]

Before leaving the convent, I made certain resolutions regarding the conduct of my life:

1. I will receive Confession and Communion each time as though it were my last.

2. I will visit Jesus in the Blessed Sacrament[3] often, especially when I am afflicted.

3. I will prepare myself for every feast of our Blessed Mother[4] by some mortification, and every evening I will ask my heavenly Mother's blessing.

4. I want to remain always in the presence of God.

---

[1] contemplation; meditation
[2] nun
[3] Holy Communion
[4] In Italy alone there are 39 yearly feast-days which honor Mary.

5. Every time the clock strikes I will repeat three times: My
   Jesus, mercy.

I would have liked to add other resolutions to these, but
my teacher would not permit it. And she had good reason,
for within a year after I returned to my family I had
forgotten these resolutions as well as the good advice I had
received, and I became worse than before. I continued to go
to school to the nuns, and they were fairly satisfied with
me. I went to Communion two or three times a week, and
Jesus made Himself felt ever stronger. Several times He
made me feel very great consolation. But as soon as I left
Him, I began to be proud, more disobedient than before, a
bad example to my companions, and a scandal to all.

At school, not a day passed on which I was not
punished. I did not know my lessons and I was almost
expelled. At home I would not let anyone have peace.
Every day I wanted to go for a walk, always wearing new
clothes which my poor father provided me for a long time. I
ceased to say my usual prayers morning and evening. But
while I was committing all these sins, I never forgot to
recite every day three Hail Mary's with my hands under my
knees (a practice my mother had taught me that Jesus might
protect me every day from sins against holy purity).

During this time, which lasted almost an entire year, the
only thing I had left was charity to the poor. Every time I
left the house I asked my father for money. If he sometimes
refused it, I would take bread, flour, or some such thing.
And God himself would see to it that I met some poor
people, for every time I left the house there would be three
or four. To those who came to the door I would give
clothes or whatever else I had.

But then my Confessor[1] forbade me to do these things,
and I stopped doing them. In this way Jesus worked in me a

---

[1] Msgr. Volpi

new conversion. For my father no longer gave me money, I could take nothing from the house, and every time I went out I met none but poor people and they all ran after me. I could not give them anything. This pained me so that I wept continually. For this reason I quit going out except when I really had to. The result was that I grew tired of clothes and everything else.

I wanted to make another general confession, but I was not permitted to do so. I did confess everything however, and Jesus gave me such a deep sorrow for my sins that I felt it always. I asked pardon of my teachers because I had displeased them most of all.

But this change did not please my father and my brothers. One brother especially chided me because I wanted to go to Mass every morning. But from then on Jesus helped me more than ever.

At this time, as my grandfather and uncle were dead, two of my aunts, my father's sisters, came to live with us. They were good, religious, and affectionate, but their affection was never the tender love of a mother. They took us to church every day and they were diligent in instructing us in the religion.

Among us brothers and sisters some were better and some worse. The oldest boy, the fourth of our family to die, and the youngest girl, Julia, were the best, and so were more loved by my aunts. But the others, who took my bad example, were far more lively and so[1] less appreciated. Nonetheless, none of us lacked what was needed.

I was always the worst of all, and who knows what a strict account I must give to the Lord for the bad example that I gave to my brothers and companions! My aunts never failed to correct me in all my failings, but I responded arrogantly, giving them many short answers.

Now, as I have said, Jesus used my prohibition to give

---

[1] therefore

alms[1] as means to convert me. I began to think of how much my sins offended Jesus. I began also to study and work harder, and my teachers continued to encourage me. The one defect for which I was often reproved and punished was my pride. My teacher frequently called me 'pride personified.'

Yes, this was my greatest sin, but only Jesus knows whether I realized it or not. Many a time I fell on my knees before my teacher and all the class, and even the Mother Superior, to beg pardon for this sin. And also many a time in the evening I wept when I was alone. I was not aware of this sin, and every day I fell into it time and again without adverting[2] to it.

The teacher who, at the time of my retreat had explained the Passion to me, reproved me one day and explained the matter to me (perhaps because she had noticed a change in me). But she did so little by little. She often said to me:

'Gemma, you belong to Jesus and you should be all His. Be good. Jesus is pleased with you, and you need much help. Meditation on the Passion ought to be something very close to your heart. Oh, if you could always be with me.'

That good teacher had detected my desire. At other times she said to me:

'Gemma, what graces Jesus has given you!'

I, who never understood all this, remained as one dumb. But sometimes I felt the need of a little talk and (I don't hesitate to say it) of a caress from my dear teacher, so I ran looking for her. Sometimes she would appear very serious, and when I saw her like that I would cry. Then she would take me into her arms (even though I was eleven years old) and caress me. As a result, I was so attached to her that I called her my mother.

---

[1] The command by her Confessor not to give to the poor.
[2] turn attention to

Every two years the nuns used to have a retreat[1] which was open also to the external students. It hardly seemed true that I could commune so intimately with Jesus again. But this time I was all alone without any help, for the nuns were making their own retreat at the same time as the children.

I understood well that Jesus was giving me this opportunity to know myself better and to purify myself and please Him more.

I recall the words which that good priest repeated so often: 'Let us remember that we are nothing and that God is all. God is our creator and all that we have He has given us.'

I remember that after a few days of the retreat, the preacher had us make a meditation on sin. It was then that I came to realize, dear Father, that I was worthy only to be despised by all. I saw myself to be so ungrateful to God, guilty as I was of so many sins.[2]

Then we made a meditation on Hell,[3] of which I knew myself to be deserving, and during this meditation I made this resolution: *I will make acts of contrition during the day, especially when I have committed some fault.*

During the last days of the retreat we considered the example of humility, meekness, obedience, and patience (of Jesus). And from this meditation I formed two more resolutions:

---

[1] The retreat was held in 1891 and during this time Gemma was to be completely changed as to give herself entirely to Jesus.

[2] The mystical teaching of Jesus can be applied here: 'The one who has been forgiven of little loves little; the one who has been forgiven of much loves much.' We have all been forgiven of much, but often our perception defaults to self-righteousness and causes us to believe that we have done little or nothing wrong—therefore we love Jesus very little as a result.

[3] *Inferno*

1. To make a visit to Jesus in the Blessed Sacrament every day and speak to Him more with the heart than with the tongue.

2. I will try harder to avoid speaking of indifferent things and to speak rather of heavenly things.

At the end of the retreat, I obtained permission from my Confessor to receive Communion three times a week, and likewise to go to confession three times a week, and I continued to do this for three or four years, until 1895.

I continued to go to school every day, but the desire to receive Jesus and to know more about his Passion increased, so much so that I succeeded in getting my teacher to explain it to me for an entire hour after every ten hours of work or study. I desired nothing else. Every day I worked or studied ten hours and spent an hour listening to the explanation of some point on the Passion. Many times as I thought of my sins and my ingratitude to Jesus, we began to weep together.

It was during these four years that this good teacher taught me also to perform some little penance for Jesus. The first was the wearing of a little rope around my body, and there were many others. But no matter how hard I tried, I never obtained the permission of my Confessor for these things. Therefore she taught me rather to mortify my eyes and my tongue. She succeeded in making me better, but with much difficulty.

This good teacher died after having led me along for six years. Then I came under the direction of another who was fully as good as the first. But she also had to reprove me often for the ugly sin of pride.[1]

---

[1] The desire to be an autonomous god outside of or separate from our Creator, which is the original sin of Adam and Eve and the same sin as the love of money (power) which, if not checked, leads to a seared

Under her direction, I began to have a great desire to pray more. Every evening as soon as school was out I would go home and shut myself up in my room and recite the entire rosary on my knees. And often I would rise during the night for about a quarter of an hour to recommend my poor soul to Jesus.

My aunts and my brothers did not pay such attention to me. They let me do whatever I wanted because they knew how bad I was. But my father always took great delight in me. He often said (and this often made me cry): 'I have only two children, Gino[1] and Gemma.'

He said such things in the presence of all the others, and, to tell the truth, we were about the most mischievous in the house.

I loved Gino more than the rest. We were always together. During vacation time we would amuse ourselves by making little altars, celebrating feasts, etc., and in this we were always alone. As he grew up, he had the desire of becoming a priest. So he was sent to seminary and put on clerical dress, but a few years later he died.

During the time when he was sick in bed, he wanted me always near him. The doctor gave up all hope for him. Since I was so sorry that he was going to die, I started using all his things so that I would die too. As a matter of fact, I almost did die. I became very seriously ill about a month later.

I cannot describe the care all lavished on me, especially my father. Many times I saw him weeping and begging Jesus to let him die in my place. He used every means possible to cure me,[2] and after three months I was well again.

---

conscience and narcissism, power madness, and every other societal and spiritual evil.

[1] This beloved brother of Gemma died of tuberculosis while he was studying for the priesthood.

[2] Her father, Enrico Galgani, was a pharmacist.

The doctor forbade me to study any more, and I quit school. Many times the superior and the nuns sent for me to come and be with them, but my father would not let me go. Every day he took me outside. He gave me everything I wanted. And I began to pamper myself once more. But I kept going to Communion three or four times a week, and even though I was so bad, Jesus came and dwelt with me and said many things to me.

I recall very well one time I was given a gold watch and chain. Ambitious as I was, I could hardly wait to put it on and go out (an indication, dear Father, that my imagination was working on me). I did, in fact, go out with it on, and when I returned and started to take it off I saw an angel (whom I recognized immediately as my Guardian Angel) who said to me very seriously: 'Remember that the precious jewelry that adorns a spouse of the Crucified King can only be thorns and the Cross.'

I did not even tell my Confessor about this. In fact, I now tell it for the first time. These words made me fear, as did the angel himself. But a little later, while reflecting on them without understanding them at all, I made this resolution: *I resolve for the love of Jesus and to please Him, never to wear the watch again and not even to speak of things that savor vanity.*

At the time I also had a ring on my finger. I took it off immediately, and from that day to this I have not worn such things.

So I resolved (because Jesus had given me clear lights to the effect that I should be a religious[1]) to change my life. I had a good occasion to do this, for we were about to begin the year of 1896. I wrote in a little notebook:

'During this new year I resolve to begin a new life. I do not know what will happen to me during this year. But I abandon myself entirely to you, my God. And my

---

[1] a monastic; a nun

74

aspirations and all my affections will be for You. I feel so weak, dear Jesus, but with Your help I hope and resolve to live a different life, that is, a life closer to You.'

From the moment when my mother inspired me with the desire for Heaven, I have always (even in the midst of so many sins) wanted it ardently. If God had left the choice to me, I would have preferred to escape from the body and fly to Heaven. Every time a fever came upon me and I felt ill, I experienced a great consolation. But this changed to sorrow when, after some illness, I would feel my strength return. One day after Holy Communion I asked Jesus why He did not take me to Heaven. He answered:

'My daughter, I do not take you because during your life I will give you many occasions to gain more merit, increasing your desire for Heaven as you bear the trials of life with patience.'

These words in no way diminished my desire. Rather I felt it increasing in me day by day.

During this same year of 1896 another desire began to grow in me. I began to feel an ever greater yearning to love Jesus Crucified very much, and at the same time a desire to suffer with Him and to help Him in his sufferings.

One day as I was looking at the crucifix, so great a sorrow came over me that I fell to the floor. My father was in the house at the time, and he began to reprove me, saying that it was not good for me to stay at home and that I should go out early the next morning (he had not let me go to Mass the last two mornings). I answered in a disturbed tone of voice: 'It is not good for me to remain away from Jesus in the Blessed Sacrament.'

My answer disturbed him because he noticed that my voice was not very strong. I hid myself in a room, and there, for the first time, I gave vent to my sorrow with Jesus alone.

Dear Father, I do not remember the words I spoke, but

my angel is here and he tells me what I said word for word. It is as follows:

'I want to follow you no matter what the cost in pain, and to follow you fervently. No, Jesus, I do not want to continue displeasing you by a tepid life as I have done up to now. That would amount to coming to you to bring you displeasure. Therefore, I resolve to make my prayer more devout and my communions more frequent. Jesus, I want to suffer, and to suffer much for you. Prayer will ever be on my lips. If even he falls often who makes frequent resolutions, what will happen to him who resolves but rarely?'

Dear Father, these words came from my heart in that moment of sorrow and of hope when I was alone with my Jesus.

I have made so many resolutions, and I never kept any of them. Every day, amid so many sins of every kind, I would ask Jesus to let me suffer, and suffer much.

After a little, Jesus sent me a consolation: He sent me a pain in one of my feet. I kept this secret for a while, but the pain was severe. A doctor came and said an operation was necessary and perhaps the foot would have to be amputated. All of my family was greatly worried, and only I was indifferent. I remember that while they were performing the operation I cried and complained loudly. But then, looking at Jesus, I begged him to pardon my folly. Jesus also sent me other pains, and I can say with truth that ever since the death of my mother I have never spent a day without suffering some little thing for Jesus.

During this time I never ceased to commit sins. I became worse every day. I was full of every kind of fault, and I do not understand why Jesus never showed himself angry with me. Only once did I see Jesus angry at me, and I would rather suffer the pains of Hell a thousand times in this life than find myself before Jesus so displeased and to see before my eyes the horrible picture of my soul as I did on the occasion of which I will speak later.

On Christmas day of 1896 I was permitted to go to Mass and receive Holy Communion. I was about fifteen years old at the time and I had already often asked my Confessor for permission to make a vow of virginity (I had asked for this for many years but I did not really know what it was; it only seemed to me that it was the most beautiful adornment I could offer to Jesus). He would not let me take this vow of virginity, but instead allowed me to make a vow of chastity.[1] So on Christmas Night I made my first vow to Jesus. I remember that Jesus was so pleased with it that He asked me after Holy Communion to unite with this vow the offering of my whole self and all my sentiments in abandonment to His holy will. I did this with such a joy that I spent that night and the next day as if in Heaven.

That year came to an end and we entered upon the year of 1897, which was a year of great sorrow for all my family. I, alone being heartless, remained unmoved in the face of so many afflictions. The thing that troubled the others the most was the fact that we were deprived of all means of livelihood, and, added to this, my father was seriously ill.

One morning after Communion I understood what a great sacrifice Jesus would ask of us soon. I wept very much, but Jesus made Himself felt in my soul all the more during those sorrowful days. I saw my father so perfectly resigned to die that I felt strong enough to bear these sorrows very calmly. On the day of his death, Jesus told me not to give way to useless weeping and wailing, so I spent the day praying in resignation to the will of God who at that moment took the role of both my heavenly and earthly father.

---

[1] The vow of virginity is the same as one of celibacy for a lifetime; the vow of chastity safeguards against thoughts and actions that sully the soul without demanding virginity in case the person has been called to one day be married.

After my father's death, we found ourselves destitute. We had only enough to live on. One of my aunts, realizing this, helped us a great deal. She was unwilling that I should remain with my family. So the day after my father's death she sent for me and had me stay with her for several months. (This was not the aunt with whom I lived after my mother's death, but another one.)

Every morning she took me to Mass, but I seldom received Communion because I could not bring myself to go to confession to anyone besides Monsignor.[1] During that time I gradually forgot Jesus once more. I neglected prayer and I began anew to seek diversions.

Another niece of my aunt who was also living with her became very friendly with me and we became very much alike in our wickedness. My aunt sent the two of us out together frequently. And I am sure that if Jesus had not had pity on my weakness I would have fallen into serious sins. Love of the world began gradually to awaken in my soul. But Jesus once more came to the rescue. All of a sudden I became stooped and began to have terrible pains in my back. I bore this for a time, but as I saw myself growing worse, I asked my aunt to take me back to Lucca. She lost no time, but sent someone back with me.

But, dear Father, the thought of those months spent in sin filled me with terror. I had committed sins of every kind. Even impure thoughts had run through my mind. I had listened to bad conversation instead of fleeing from it. I had told untruths to my aunt to protect my companion. In short, I had stood on the brink of Hell.

Once again at Lucca, I was better for some time. I never wanted to obey when they wished a doctor to visit me (for I never wanted anyone to touch me or see me.) One evening a doctor came unannounced, examined me by force, and found an abscess on my body which he feared was very

---

[1] Volpi

serious because he thought it had affected my spine.

For a long time I had felt pain in that part of my body, but I did not want to touch or look at it because when I was a little girl I had heard a priest say: 'Our body is the temple of the Holy Spirit.' Those words had struck me and led me to guard my body as closely as possible.

After he had visited me, the doctor called a consultant. What affliction it caused me, dear Father, to have to uncover myself. Every time the doctor touched me I cried. After the consultation I grew steadily worse and I was forced to go to bed and was not able to move. Every remedy was used on me, but instead of helping me they made me worse. While I was in bed, I was ill at ease and a source of annoyance to all.

The second day I was in bed, I was not at peace and I wrote to Monsignor telling him that I wanted to see him. He came at once and I made a general confession, not indeed because I was so bad off but to regain peace of conscience which I had lost. After confession my peace with Jesus returned, and as a sign of this, on that same evening I experienced a very deep sorrow for my sins.

Then, dear Father, the pain became worse and worse and the doctors decided to operate on me (in that part of which I have spoken). Three doctors came (and what I suffered from the pain was as nothing). I felt pain and suffering only when I found myself in their presence almost entirely unclothed. Dear Father, how much better it would have been for me to die! Finally the doctors saw that all remedies were useless, and they gave me up entirely. After that they came to see me only now and then through courtesy, so to speak.

Regarding the nature of this illness, nearly all the doctors said it was a spinal disease and only one insisted that it was hysteria. I had to lie in one position in bed and it was impossible for me to move myself. In order to have a little relief now and then I had to ask some of the family to help me to move an arm, now a leg. They took excellent care of me, but I, on the contrary, repaid them only with bad manners and short answers.

One evening, when I was more uncomfortable than usual, I was complaining to Jesus, telling Him that I would not have prayed so much if I had known He was not going to cure me, and I asked Him why He wanted me to be sick this way. My angel answered me as follows:

'If Jesus afflicts you in body it is always in order to purify your soul. Be good.'

Oh, how many times during my long illness did I not experience consoling words in my heart! But I never profited by them.

The thing that afflicted me most was to have to stay in bed, because I wanted to do what the others were doing. I wanted to go to confession every day and to Mass each morning. But one morning when they brought Holy Communion to me at home, Jesus made Himself felt rather strongly in my soul and He gave me a severe rebuke, telling me that I was a weak soul.

'It is your bad self-love that makes you resent not being able to do what the others do,' He said to me, 'and that causes you so much confusion at seeing that you have to be helped by others. If you were dead to yourself you would not be so disturbed.'

During this time my family was making triduums[1] and novenas[2] and having others make them for my cure. But they obtained nothing. I myself remained indifferent. The words of Jesus had strengthened but not converted me.

One day a lady who often came to visit me brought me a book to read (*The Life of Venerable Gabriel*). I took it almost disdainfully and put it on the pillow. The lady begged me to recommend myself to Gabriel, but I thought

---

[1] prayers for three days
[2] prayers for nine days

little of it. My family, however, began to say three Paters, Aves, and Gloria's in his honor every day.

One day I was alone. It was a little after noon. I was attacked by a strong temptation, and I said within myself that I was tired of all this, and staying in bed annoyed me. The devil took advantage of these thoughts and began to tempt me, saying that if I had listened to him he would have cured me and would have done all that I asked of him. Dear Father, I was on the point of giving in. I was disturbed and felt that I was conquered. But suddenly a thought came to me. My mind turned to Venerable Gabriel and I said fervently: 'The soul comes first and then the body!'

Nevertheless the devil continued with even stronger assaults. A thousand ugly thoughts rushed through my mind. Again I turned to Venerable Gabriel, and with his help I conquered. Entering within myself, I made the Sign of the Cross, and in a quarter of an hour I turned to unite myself with God, Whom I so little appreciated. I recall that on that very evening I began to read the life of Brother Gabriel. I read it several times. I never grew tired of reading it and admiring his virtues and his example. My resolutions were many, my deeds but few.

From the day on which my new protector, Venerable Gabriel, saved my soul, I began to practice a special devotion to him. At night I could not sleep unless I had his picture under my pillow. And from that day to this I began to see him near me (here, dear Father, I do not know how to express myself; I have felt his presence). In every act, in every bad action that I have performed, I thought of Brother Gabriel and thereupon ceased the action. I have never failed to pray to him every day in these words: 'The soul comes before the body.'

One day the lady who had brought me the life of Venerable Gabriel came to take it back. In taking it from under my pillow and giving it back to her, I could not help weeping. The lady, seeing that it was so hard for me to give it up, promised to come back later and get it when the person who had given it to her requested it. She came back a few days later and I had to give it back to her, though I did so weeping. This caused me much displeasure.

But that Saint of God very soon rewarded this little sacrifice, for that night in a dream he appeared to me clothed in white. I did not recognize him, dear Father. When he saw that I did not recognize him, he opened the white garment and I saw him clothed as a Passionist. I knew him immediately. I remained in silence before him. He asked me why I had cried when they took his life[1] from me. I don't recall what I answered, but he said:

'See how much your sacrifice has pleased me. It has pleased me so much that I have come myself to see you. Do you wish me well?' I did not answer. Then he comforted me and said to me: 'Be good, because I will return to see you.' He told me to kiss his habit and rosary,[2] and then he went away.

My imagination started working, and I found myself always awaiting another visit from him. But he did not come again for many, many months.

Here is how it happened. The feast of the Immaculate Conception came. At that time the Brabantine nuns, Sisters of Charity, were coming to change my clothing and tend to me. Among those who came, there was one who was not yet vested in the habit and who was not vested until two years later because she was too young. On the vigil of the feast, the nuns came as usual, and while they were there I had an inspiration. I thought within myself: 'Tomorrow is the feast of our Blessed Mother. If I should promise her that if she would cure me I would become a Sister of Charity, what would happen?'

This thought consoled me. I told it to Sister Leonilda

---

[1] the book about his life and deeds
[2] Acts of contrition to instill in Gemma the need for humility—this is not saint worship or anything of the sort.

82

and she promised that if I were cured I could be vested with the novice of whom I spoke above. All that remained was that I should make the promise the next morning after Holy Communion. Monsignor came to hear my confession, and he immediately gave his permission. He also gave me another consolation. We made a perpetual vow of virginity together that evening, a vow which previously he had never allowed me to make. He renewed it[1] and I made it for the first and last time. What tremendous graces, but I have never corresponded[2] with them!

That evening I was in perfect peace. Night came and I went to sleep. All of a sudden I saw my Protector[3] standing before me at the foot of my bed. He said to me: 'Gemma, make the vow to become a religious gladly, but add nothing else.'

'But why!' I asked.

Touching me on the forehead while he looked at me and smiled, he answered: 'My sister!'

I did not understand what it was all about. To thank him, I kissed his habit. He took the woolen heart (which Passionists wear on their breast), had me kiss it, and then placed it on the sheet over my heart, and again said to me: 'My sister!' With that he disappeared.

The next morning there was nothing on the sheet. I went to Communion, and afterwards made my promise,[4] but added nothing else. I did not speak of this either with the nuns or with my Confessor. At that time, and many times later, the nuns reminded me of my vow because they thought I had promised to become a Sister of Charity, and they told me that our Blessed Mother could cure me. Jesus graciously accepted my vow, and my poor heart was very

---

[1] renewed his
[2] become parallel or matched with ('I have never come up to their standard!')
[3] Venerable Gabriel
[4] to become a nun, but of no specific order or rule

83

glad.

But the months passed and I did not get any better. On the fourth of January the doctors tried another remedy. They cauterized me in twelve places along the spine.[1] That was enough. I began to grow worse.[2] Besides the usual pains, on January 28th I began to suffer an unbearable headache. The doctor whom they called said that it was very dangerous (calling it a tumor of the brain). They could not operate because I was suffering from extreme weakness. I grew worse from day to day, and on the Second of February they brought me Holy Viaticum.[3] I made my confession, and I was waiting to go and be with Jesus. It seemed that it would be soon. The doctors, thinking that I was no longer conscious, said among themselves that I would not live until midnight. Live Jesus!

One of my teachers in school (of whom I have spoken above) came to see me and to tell me farewell, saying that she would see me in Heaven. But nonetheless she begged me to make a novena to Blessed Margaret Mary Alacoque,[4] assuring me that she would gain for me the grace either of being cured perfectly, or else of entering Heaven immediately after death.

This teacher, before she would leave my bed, made me promise her to begin the novena that same evening. It was February 18th. I did begin it. That very evening I said the prayers for the first time. The next day I forgot them. On the 20th I began all over again, but once more I forgot to say the prayers. This was very poor attention to prayer, was

---

[1] The medical technique of burning a part of the body to remove, close off, or in some way heal it.

[2] Here we see Gemma's dry sense of humor indicating her happy resolve to suffer for Jesus and sinners.

[3] Holy Communion administered to the dying.

[4] A nun and mystic who promoted devotion to the Sacred Heart of Jesus, 1647-1690.

it not, dear Father?[1]

On the 23rd I began for the third time (that is, I intended to), but a little before midnight I heard a rosary rattling and I felt a hand resting on my forehead. I heard someone begin saying the Pater, Ave, and Gloria, and repeating them nine times. I could hardly answer the prayers because my pain was so intense. Then that same voice that had said the prayers asked me: 'Do you want to be cured?' 'It's all the same to me,' I answered.

'Yes,' he said. 'You will be cured. Pray with faith[2] to the Heart of Jesus. Every evening until the novena is finished I will be here with you and we will pray to the Heart of Jesus together.'

'And Blessed Margaret Mary?' I asked. 'You may add three Gloria's in her honor.'

The same thing happened for nine successive nights. The same person came every evening, placed his hand on my forehead, and we recited together the prayers of the Sacred Heart, after which he had me add three Gloria's in honor of Bl. Margaret Mary.

It was the second to last day of the novena, and I wanted to receive Communion on the last day which was the first Friday of March. I sent for my Confessor and went to confession. The next morning I received Communion. What happy moments I spent with Jesus! He kept repeating to me: 'Gemma, do you want to be cured?' I was so moved that I could not answer. Poor Jesus! The grace had been given. I was cured.

'My daughter,' Jesus said embracing me, 'I give Myself entirely to you and you will be entirely Mine.' I saw clearly that Jesus had taken my parents from me, and sometimes this made me discouraged, because I believed myself abandoned. That morning I complained to Jesus about this

---

[1] Desire intact, will (discipline) once again neglected.
[2] trust

and He, always so good and tender, said to me: 'My daughter, I will always be with you. I will be your father and she (indicating our Mother of Sorrows) will be your mother. He who is My hands can never lack fatherly help. You will never lack anything even though I have taken away from you all earthly consolation and support. Come, draw near to me, you are My daughter. Are you not happy to be the daughter of Jesus and Mary?' The overwhelming affections to which Jesus gave rise in my heart kept me from answering.

After about two hours had passed I arose. Those in the house wept for joy. I too was happy, not because I was cured but because Jesus had chosen me to be His daughter. Before leaving me that morning, Jesus said to me: 'To the grace that has been given you this morning there will be added many more and greater ones.' And this has been so true, because Jesus has always protected me in a special way. I have treated Him only with coldness and indifference, and in exchange He has given me only signs of infinite love.

From that time on I could hardly bear not to receive Jesus every morning. But I was not able to do so. I had the permission of my Confessor to do so, but I was so weak that I could hardly stand on my feet. On the second Friday of March 1899, I went to church for the first time to receive Holy Communion. And from then until now I have continued to go every day. I missed only now and then because my great sins made me unworthy, or as a chastisement imposed on me by my Confessor.

That same morning, the second Friday of March, the Visitandine Sisters wanted to see me. I went to see them and they promised me that in May I could come to them and make a course of spiritual exercises. Furthermore, they told me that if my desire proved to be a true vocation, they would take me into the convent in June for good. I felt great contentment in the thought of this, especially since

Monsignor was in perfect accord with the idea.

The month of March passed with me receiving Communion every morning, and Jesus was filling me with unspeakable consolations. Then came Holy Week. I wanted so much to attend the sacred functions. But Jesus had arranged otherwise. During the Holy Week, He asked of me a great sacrifice. Wednesday of Holy Week came (no sign had been given me except that when I received Communion Jesus made Himself felt in a most wonderful manner).

From the moment when I got up from my sick bed, my Guardian Angel began to be my master and guide. He corrected me every time I did something wrong, and he taught me to speak but little, and that only when I was spoken to. One day when those in the house were speaking of some person and were not speaking very well of her, I wanted to speak up but the angel gave me a severe rebuke. He taught me to keep my eyes cast down, and one time in church he reproved me strongly saying to me: 'Is this the way to conduct yourself in the presence of God?' And another time he chided me in this way: 'If you are not good I will not let you see me anymore.' He taught me many times how to act in the presence of God; that is, to adore Him in His infinite goodness, His infinite majesty, His mercy, and in all His attributes.

As I said before, we were in Holy Week. It was Wednesday. My Confessor had finally decided that it would be well for me to make a general confession as I had desired for so long a time. He chose a late hour on Wednesday for me to do this. In His infinite mercy, Jesus gave me a very deep sorrow for my sins, and here is how it came about.

On Thursday evening I began to make the Holy Hour. (I had promised the Sacred Heart that if I were cured I would make the Holy Hour every Thursday without fail.) This was the first time I had made it out of bed. I had made it on the preceding Thursdays, but in bed because my Confessor would not let me make it any other way on account of my extreme weakness. But from the time of my general confession he permitted me to make it out of bed.

I began therefore, to make the Holy Hour, but I felt myself so full of sorrow for my sins that it was a time of continual martyrdom. However, in the midst of this sorrow there was one comfort, namely, weeping. This was both a comfort and a relief to me. I spent the entire hour praying and weeping. Finally, being very tired, I sat down, but the sorrow continued. I became entirely recollected, and after a little bit, all of a sudden I felt my strength fail. (It was only with great difficulty that I was able to get up and lock the door to the room.) Where was I? Dear Father, I found myself before Jesus Crucified. He was bleeding all over. I lowered my eyes and the sight filled me with pain. I made the Sign of the Cross and immediately my anguish was succeeded by peace of soul. I continued to feel an even stronger sorrow for my sins and I had not the courage to raise my eyes and look at Jesus. I prostrated myself on the floor and remained there for several hours. 'My daughter,' He said. 'Behold these wounds. They have all been opened for your sins. But now, be consoled, for they have all been closed by your sorrow. Do not offend Me anymore. Love Me as I have always loved you. Love Me.' This He repeated several times.

The vision vanished, and I returned to my senses. From that time on I began to have a great horror for sin (which was the greatest grace Jesus has given me). The wounds of Jesus remained so vividly impressed in my mind that they have never been effaced.

On the morning of Good Friday, I received Holy Communion, and I would have liked to have gone to the services that day in honor of the Agony. But my family would not permit it even though I wept. With great difficulty I made this first sacrifice to Jesus. And Jesus,

88

always so generous, saw fit to reward me even though I made the sacrifice with much difficulty. I shut myself in my room, therefore, to make the hour of Agony alone. But I was not alone. My Guardian Angel came to me and we prayed together. We assisted Jesus in all His sufferings, and compassionated our Mother in her sorrows. But my angel did not fail to give me a gentle rebuke, telling me that I should not cry when I had to make a sacrifice to Jesus; but, that I should rather thank those who offered me the occasion to do so.

This was the first time, and also the first Friday on which Jesus made Himself felt so strongly in my soul. And although I did not receive Communion from the hands of a priest because it was impossible, Jesus nevertheless came Himself and communicated Himself to me.[1] And this union with Him was so overwhelming that I remained as if stupefied.

Jesus spoke very strongly to me. 'What are you doing?' He said to me. 'What have you to say? Aren't you ever moved at all?'

Then it was that, not being able to resist any longer, I blurted out: 'Oh Jesus, how is it that You Who are most perfect and all holy choose one so full of coldness and imperfection to love?'

He answered: 'I am burning with desire to unite myself with you. Hasten to receive Me every morning. But remember that I am a father and a zealous spouse. Will you be My daughter and My faithful spouse?'

I made a thousand promises to Jesus that morning but, my God, how soon I forgot them! I always felt a horror for sin, but at the same time I was always committing it. And Jesus was not satisfied with me though He ever consoled me, sending my Guardian Angel to be my guide in everything.

---

[1] The very essence of Holy Communion.

After these things happened to me, I felt that I should speak to my Confessor about them. I went to confession, but I did not have the courage. I left the confessional without saying anything about it. I returned home, and on entering my room I noticed that my angel was weeping. I didn't have the courage to ask him what he was crying about, but he himself told me. 'Do you want to be deprived of seeing me anymore? You are a bad girl. You are hiding things from your Confessor. Remember this, and I am telling you for the last time, if you ever hide anything else from your Confessor, I will never let you see me anymore. Never, never.'

I fell to my knees, and he told me to make an act of contrition and made me promise to reveal everything to my Confessor. With this he pardoned me in the Name of Jesus.

The month of April had arrived. I was impatiently awaiting the time when I could go to the Visitandine Sisters to make a retreat as they had promised me. One time, it was one morning after Communion, Jesus told me about something that had displeased Him very much. I had committed the fault the evening before.

Two young girls who were friends of one of my sisters used to come to our house, and though their conversation was not bad, it was worldly. This time I took part in the conversation, adding my little bit like the others. But the next morning Jesus rebuked me so severely that it inspired in me a great terror, and I would have desired never to see or speak to anyone else.

Nevertheless, Jesus continued to make Himself felt in my soul every day, filling me with consolation. And I, on the other hand, continued to turn my back to Him and offend Him without any sorrow.

Two sentiments were engendered in my heart after the first time Jesus made Himself felt and allowed me to see Him covered with blood. The first was to love Him even to the point of sacrifice. But since I did not know how to love

Him truly, I asked my Confessor to teach me and he answered as follows:

'How do we learn to read and write? We practice reading and writing over and over until we finally learn how.'

This answer did not convince me. In fact, I didn't know what he meant. Often I asked him the same question, but he always gave me the same answer.

The other sentiment that sprung up in my heart after having seen Jesus was a desire to suffer something for Him, seeing that He had suffered so much for me. I got myself a thick rope which I took secretly from the well, made several knots in it, and put it around my body. But I didn't have it on a quarter of an hour before my Guardian Angel reproved me and made me take it off because I had not asked my Confessor's permission and obtained it. But my great affliction was not being able to love Jesus as I wished. I tried eagerly not to offend Him, but my bad inclination to evil was so strong that without a special grace of God I would have fallen into Hell.

Not knowing how to love Jesus caused me much concern but He, in His infinite goodness, was never ashamed to humiliate me in order that He might become my Master. One evening when I was at prayer He came to bring peace to my soul. I felt myself entirely recollected, and I found myself a second time before Jesus Crucified. He said to me:

'Look daughter, and learn how to love,' and He showed me his five open wounds. 'Do you see this cross, these thorns, these nails, these bruises, these tears, these wounds, this blood? They are all works of love, and of infinite love. Do you see how much I have loved you? Do you really want to love Me? Then first learn to suffer. It is by suffering that one learns to love.'

On seeing this, I experienced a new sorrow, and thinking of the infinite love of Jesus for us and the sufferings He had undergone for our salvation, I fell fainting to the floor, and I remained thus for several hours. All that had happened to me during these times of prayer brought me such great consolation that, although they were prolonged for several hours, I was not tired out.

I continued to make the Holy Hour every Thursday, but sometimes it happened that it lasted until about two o'clock because I was with Jesus and almost always He gave me a share in the grief that He experienced in the garden at the sight of my many sins and those of the entire world. It was such a deep sorrow that it could well be compared to the agony of death. After all this I would experience so sweet a calm and consolation that I had to give vent to it in tears. And these tears made me taste an incomprehensible love, and increased in me the desire to love Jesus and to suffer for Him.

The time of the retreat I wanted so much was drawing near, and on the first of May, 1899, at three o'clock I went into the convent. I felt that I was entering Heaven itself. What consolations! For the first time I forbade those of my family to come to see me during that time because those days were all for Jesus. On the evening that I entered, Monsignor came and granted me the permission (as the Mother Superior desired) that I should not make the retreat in private but that I should make it as a kind of test, that is, doing all that the nuns did. This consoled me in one way, but in another way it displeased me because that way I could not be as recollected.[1] But I wanted to obey without a word. The Mother Superior put the Mistress of Novices in charge of me. She gave me a schedule to follow while I was there.

I had to rise at five o'clock, go to the choir at 5:30, receive Holy Communion and then recite Prime and Sext[2]

---

[1] contemplative
[2] Two of the 'little hours' of the Roman Catholic church.

with the nuns. Then I would leave the choir to take breakfast and a half hour later go to my cell. At nine o'clock I would go to the choir again for the community Mass and to recite None. Then, at 9:30 Monsignor would come to give me a little conference if he could. But when he could not come, I would make a meditation from a book that he sent me during that time and then he would come in the evening to give me a little talk. At 10:15 when the meditation was over, I would make a visit to Jesus with the nuns. From 10:30 until 11:30 was the dinner hour and from then until 12:30 we had recreation (I had permission from Monsignor to spend only one recreation period a day with the nuns because I wanted to spend the evening recreation in the choir with Jesus). At 12:30 I went to the novitiate where there was work until three o'clock. At three we went again to the choir to recite Vespers, and then the community gathered for an instruction from the superior until five o'clock. At five we went again to the choir to recite Compline which was followed by an hour of meditation which we made in any manner we pleased. After meditation we went to the refectory[1] again and then to recreation. This recreation period I spent with the superior in her room or else in the choir. At 8:30 the community gathered again for about a half hour and at 9:00 we recited Matins and went to bed.

Dear Father, it seemed to me that this type of life was almost too easy for the nuns, and rather than becoming attached to it, I began instead to dislike that manner of life. The novices, who all had special concern for me, would advise me now and then and speak of those things which were more appealing about the community, but I gave no thought to these things. The thing that afflicted me was the thought that I had to return to the world. I would have preferred to remain there (even though that form of life did

---

[1] dining room

93

not appeal to me) than return again to those places where there were many occasions of offending Jesus. I begged Monsignor to grant me the permission to remain at the convent.

With the permission of the Mother Superior and the entire community, I asked permission of the Archbishop to remain there, but he would not grant it, saying that my health was still so poor that I was wearing an iron brace on my back to hold it straight (I haven't the slightest idea who told the Archbishop). The Mother Superior commanded me under obedience, therefore, to take off the brace. I wept on receiving this command because I well knew that I could not do without it. I ran to the novitiate and prayed to my dear Child Jesus. Then I hastened to my room. I took it off, and though nearly two years have passed since then, I have never worn it again and I am doing very well.

The superior, on hearing of this, hastened to tell the Monsignor that he might inform the Archbishop. There was only one more day left of the retreat, and Monsignor came to hear my confession. He asked me if I would remain in the convent for twelve more days because on May 21 some of the Sisters were going to make their profession and they wanted me to be present.

I was infinitely happy to remain with them, but I was convinced of one thing: that life was too easy for me. I had sinned so much that I must do penance. I revealed my fears to Jesus after Communion and Jesus, ever considering my misery, consoled me and made Himself felt in my soul, quieting me with consoling words. I was present, as Monsignor wished, at the profession of four novices. That morning I wept very much. Jesus was closer to me than usual, and some of the Sisters who saw me came up to me and asked if I needed anything because I was at the point of losing my senses. (It was true. The nuns had forgotten to give me breakfast and they hadn't given me my dinner[1] yet, so that I ate only after one o'clock).

But I received a stiff rebuke for this, as I deserved. I should have gone to the refectory on my own when the bell rang. But I was ashamed or rather, (listen, dear Father to what limit my malice, or rather my human respect, leads me) the Mother Superior always kept me beside her wherever we were. But that day of Profession the newly professed nuns took their place alongside the Superior so that I remained outside without eating. My pride would not allow me to take second place to them.

My God, I merited worse, but Jesus still supported me. He chastised me by not making Himself felt for several days. I wept much on account of this, but Jesus sent my Guardian Angel to me again and he said to me: 'Happy you, daughter, who deserve such a just punishment.' I understood none of these words, but they brought consolation to my heart.

My God! There came another sorrow. The next day I had to leave the convent and return home. I wanted that day never to come, but it was at hand. At five o'clock in the afternoon on May 21, 1899, I had to leave. In tears, I asked the blessing of the Mother Superior, said good-bye to the nuns, and left. My God! What grief!

But an even greater sorrow was to follow soon on this one. I returned to my family, but I was no longer able to adapt myself. My mind and heart were fixed on the idea of becoming a religious, and no one could discourage me from it. In order to leave the world, I seriously considered becoming a Visitandine Nun at once. Almost every day I would hasten to the monastery and the sisters promised me that in the month of June, on the feast of the Sacred Heart, they would accept me.

I must say, however, that my heart was not fully at rest

---

[1] The midday meal.

because I knew that the Visitandine life was too easy for me. And many times, on different occasions, Jesus said to me in my heart: 'Daughter, you need a more austere rule.'[1] But I very seldom paid any attention to these words and I remained firm in resolution.

We began the month of June, and I noticed that the nuns were changing their attitude. Every time I went to see the Superior, they told me that she could not come, and she would send first one then another to talk to me. They began to speak seriously to me, telling me that unless I could bring at least four medical certificates with me I would not be accepted. I tried to fulfill this requirement, but all efforts were in vain. The doctors would not cooperate, and one day the nuns told me that when I brought the certificates, they would receive me immediately, but until then absolutely not. This decision did not disturb me in the least because Jesus was consoling me with so many graces.

On the 8th of June after Communion, Jesus told me that in that evening He would give me a very great grace. I went that same day to confession, and I told Monsignor about it. He told me to be very attentive so that I could tell him all about it afterwards.

Evening came and all of a sudden, earlier than usual, I felt an interior sorrow for my sins far deeper than I had ever experienced before. In fact, it brought me very, very close to death. After this, all the powers of my soul became recollected. My intellect could think of nothing but my sins and the offense they gave to God. My memory recalled all my sins to mind and made me see all the torments that Jesus had suffered in order to save me. And my will made me detest them and promise to be willing to suffer anything in order to expiate[2] them. My mind was flooded with

---

[1] The 'rule' is the written and strictly adhered to way of life for a monk or nun of any one of the many religious paths of the Roman Catholic church.
[2] amend for; atone

thoughts— thoughts of sorrow, of love, of fear, of hope, and of comfort.

Following on this interior recollection, I was quickly rapt out of my senses, and I found myself before my heavenly Mother. At her right stood my Guardian Angel who told me to make an act of contrition. When I had finished it, my blessed Mother said to me: 'Daughter, in the Name of Jesus all your sins are forgiven.' Then she added: 'Jesus my Son loves you very much, and He wants to give you a grace. Do you know how to make yourself worthy of it?' In my misery I did not know what to answer. She continued: 'I will be your Mother. Will you be a true daughter?' She spread her mantle and covered me with it.

At that moment Jesus appeared with all His wounds open. But blood no longer came out of those wounds. Rather, flames as of fire issued forth from them, and in a moment those flames came to touch my hands, feet, and heart. I felt as if I would die. I fell to the floor. But my Mother supported me, keeping me covered with her mantle. I had to remain for several hours in that position. Then the Blessed Mother kissed me on the forehead, and it all disappeared and I found myself kneeling on the floor. But I still felt an intense pain in my hands, feet, and heart.

I arose to lie down on the bed and I noticed that blood was flowing from those places where I felt pain. I covered these parts as best I could and then, with the help of my angel, I was able to get in bed. These sufferings and pains, although they afflicted me, filled me with perfect peace. The next morning I was able to go to Communion only with great difficulty, and I put on a pair of gloves in order to hide my hands. I could hardly stand on my feet, and I thought I would die any minute. The sufferings continued until three o'clock Friday afternoon, the solemn feast of the Sacred Heart of Jesus.

I should have told these things to my Confessor at once, but instead I went to confession several times without saying anything about them. He asked me about it several times, but I would not tell him.

Meanwhile, some time passed and every Thursday about eight o'clock I began to feel the usual sufferings. And every time this happened to me, I first felt a deep and intense sorrow for my sins. This caused me more suffering than the pains in my hands, feet, head, and heart. This sorrow for my sins reduced me to a state of grief close to death. But in spite of this wonderful grace from God, I did not improve, but rather I committed numerous sins every day. I was disobedient and insincere with my Confessor, always hiding something or other from him. My angel admonished me many times, telling me that if I continued to do this he would not allow me to see him anymore. But I did not obey him, and he did go away, or rather, he would only hide himself for a while.

During this time, my desire to become a nun kept increasing. I told my Confessor about this, but he gave me little consolation. I spoke to Jesus about it, and one morning when I felt this desire more strongly than usual, Jesus said to me: 'Daughter, what are you afraid of? Hide this desire in My heart and no one will be able to take it away.' Jesus spoke to me in this way because, since this desire to go to the convent and unite myself forever with Jesus was so great, I feared someone would be able to take it away from me. But Jesus immediately consoled me with these words and others that I have forgotten.

Jesus never failed to make himself felt and seen, especially when I was afflicted. One day (which deserves special mention) I had been scolded, as I always deserved, by one of my brothers because I was going out for a while to pray in the church. During the little dispute that we had, I suffered a slight blow, which I deserved, and I was complaining about it. Jesus was not at all pleased, and He reproved me with certain words which truly hurt me. He said: 'Daughter, are you also adding your share to the pain of my Heart? I have exalted you to be My daughter and honored you with the title of My servant, and now how do you behave? You are an arrogant daughter, and unfaithful servant. You are bad!'

These words made such an impression on my heart that even though Jesus added new crosses after that, He always gave me the strength to thank Him, and not to complain anymore.

Jesus gave me an even stronger rebuke one time in these words, which at that time I did not understand but I later found them to be true. He said:

'Daughter, you complain too much in adversity, you are too perplexed in temptation and too timid to control your affections. I give you nothing but love: love in adversity, in prayer, in affronts, love in everything. And tell me, daughter, can you deny Me such a just satisfaction and such a little recompense?'[1]

I could not find words to answer Jesus. My heart almost burst with sorrow, and I said the following words which I remember so well:

'My heart, O Jesus, is ready to do everything. It is ready to burst with sorrow if You will it, my God!'

The month of June was almost over, and near the end of the month a mission began in the church of St. Martin. I always preferred to miss the mission rather than miss the sermons on the Sacred Heart at the Visitation church. But finally the latter ended and I began to go to hear the mission sermons in St. Martin Church. I cannot describe the impression made on me when I saw those priests preach! The impression was very great because I saw that they were clothed with the same kind of habit that Brother Gabriel was wearing the first time I saw him. I was seized with such an affection for them that I never missed a sermon from that day until the end of the mission.

---

[1] reward; payback

The last day of the mission arrived, and all the people were gathered in the church for the general Communion. I was among the large crowd and Jesus, who was greatly pleased, made Himself strongly felt by my soul and He said to me:

'Gemma, do you like the habit that priest is wearing?' (He indicated a Passionist who was somewhat distant from me.) I did not answer with words, but my heart answered him with its palpitations. He added: 'Would you like to be clothed with the same habit?'

'My God!' I exclaimed. 'Yes.'

Jesus continued, 'You will be a daughter of my Passion, and a well-beloved daughter. One of these sons (of the Passion) will be your father. Go and reveal everything.' And I saw that Jesus indicated Father Ignatius.

I obeyed. On the last day of the mission I went to church, but no matter how hard I tried I could hardly bring myself to speak of the affairs of my soul. Instead of going to Father Ignatius, I went to Father Cajetan and with great difficulty I told him about all that had happened to me as I have here related. He listened to me with infinite patience and he promised he would return to Lucca the following Monday and then he would have more time for my confession. Such was the arrangement. A week later I was able to go to confession to him again, and I continued to go to him the next few times.[1]

At this time, and by means of this priest, I made the acquaintance of a lady to whom I have to this day the love of a mother and whom I have always regarded as such.

The only reason I went to confession to this priest[2] was this: my ordinary Confessor[3] had forbidden me many times

---

[1] She blatantly disobeys Jesus by going to a different priest than the one He pointed out to her, but we all do similar things—to our shame.
[2] Father Cajetan
[3] Msgr. Volpi

to make the three vows of chastity, obedience, and poverty[1] because it would be impossible to observe them as long as I remained in the world.[2] I, who had always had a great desire to make them, made use of that occasion, and this was the first thing I asked of him. He immediately gave me the permission to make them from the 5th of July to the solemn feast of the 8th of September, and then they were to be renewed. I was very happy at this, and it became one of my greatest consolations. At the cost of great patience on the part of this priest, and with great shame on my part, I revealed everything to him. I told him of all the particular graces the Lord had given me, the visits from my Guardian Angel, the presence of Jesus, and also some penances which of my own accord and without any permission I had been performing every day. He at once commanded me to cease doing these things, and he took from me some of the instruments of penance that I had been using. Then this priest spoke clearly to me and told me that he was not in a position to direct me properly and that I must reveal everything to my Confessor.

I was in no way minded to follow this advice because I foresaw a great struggle and I feared the danger of being abandoned by Monsignor on account of my lack of sincerity and confidence in him. On no condition would I tell this priest the name of my Confessor. I told him that I did not know who he was and I might have even invented a false name. I don't remember. But my little trick did not go far. To my great shame, I was discovered. Father Cajetan

---

[1] Based upon the three temptations of Jesus when he fasted for 40 Jewish days (each day being 12 hours) or 20 days, the limit for any human to go without food. Poverty safeguards the body, Chastity safeguards the soul, and Obedience safeguards the spirit. An in-depth study on this most important topic reveals many priceless gems of wisdom. For example, when Queen Jezebel was thrown from her window, the dogs ate everything excepts her head, hands, and feet— symbolizing that she was unclean in spirit, soul, and body.
[2] Impossible for some, possible for others.

knew that Monsignor was my Confessor, but he could not
speak to him about me unless I gave him permission.
Finally, after keeping him in suspense for a while, I gave
him permission and it turned out that the two of them were
in complete agreement. Monsignor gave me permission to
go to this Father to confession whenever I wished and did
not scold me as I had indeed deserved. I told Monsignor
about the vows I had made, and he approved of them,
adding to them a fourth vow, namely, sincerity with my
Confessor. He further commanded me to remain hidden
and to speak of the affairs of my soul to no one but himself.

Meanwhile the Friday occurrences continued and
Monsignor thought it well to have a doctor visit me during
one of them without my knowing it. But Jesus warned me
saying: 'Tell your Confessor that in the presence of the
doctor I will do none of the things that he desires.'
Following the advice of Jesus, I told my Confessor about
this, but he did as he had planned, and events turned out as
Jesus had said, as you already know.

Dear Father, from that day a new life began for me and I
could tell you many things here, but, Jesus willing, I will
tell them to you when we are alone (in the confessional).

This was the first and best humiliation that Jesus gave
me. Nevertheless, my great pride and self-love resented it.
But Jesus, in His infinite charity,[1] continued to give me His
graces and favors. One day Jesus lovingly said to me (dear
Father, because Jesus spoke these words to me I will tell
them to you alone, but maybe you will understand them
without me explaining them):

'Daughter, what can I say when you, in all your doubts,
afflictions, and adversities think always of yourself instead
of Me? When you always hasten to find some relief and
comfort rather than turn to Me?'

Dear Father, do you understand? This was a just rebuke

---

[1] *agape* or 'love of God'

from Jesus, one that I knew I well deserved. But nonetheless I continued as usual, and Jesus again reproved me saying:

'Gemma, do you think that I am not offended when in your great needs you turn to things that cannot bring you consolation instead of turning to Me? I suffer, daughter, when I see you forget Me.'

This last reproof was enough for me, and it succeeded in detaching me entirely from every creature in order to seek my Creator in everything.

I received another prohibition from my Confessor regarding the extraordinary experiences on Thursdays and Fridays,[1] and Jesus obeyed for a little while. But then they returned as formerly, and even more so. I was no longer afraid to reveal everything (to my Confessor), and he told me emphatically that if he was not allowed to see these things, clearly he would not believe in such fantasies. Without losing any time, that very day I said a special prayer to Jesus in the Blessed Sacrament for this intention. And behold! As often happened to me, I felt myself become interiorly recollected and soon I was rapt out of my senses. I found myself before Jesus, but He was not alone. Standing beside Him was a man with white hair, and from his habit I knew that he was a Passionist. He had his hands joined and he was praying, praying fervently. As I looked at him, Jesus said to me:

'Daughter, do you know him?'

I told him 'No,' as was true.

'Look,' he added. 'That priest will be your director, and it will be he who will recognize in you, miserable creature, the infinite work of my mercy.'

After this happened, I thought no more of it. But one day I chanced to see a little portrait. It was without a doubt a picture of the priest that I had seen beside Jesus, though

---

[1] She was told that these ecstasies and visions could not continue.

the likeness was very poor. Dear Father, my intimate union with you in prayer began from the moment when I first saw you with Jesus in my vision. From then on I always wanted to have you with me, but the more I desired it, the more it seemed impossible. From that day on I would pray many times a day for this, and after several months Jesus consoled me by having you come to see me. Now I will say no more, because from that time until now you have always known me and you know everything.

—*Gemma*

A Biographical Sketch *of*

Gemma Galgani

Anonymous

[dated ca. early 20th Century]

Gemma was a layperson[1] whose life was marked
throughout by divine favors and extraordinary graces, and
also great trials and sufferings. Though she was an
extraordinary mystic and stigmatic, bearing in her body the
marks of the Lord Jesus, her spiritual life was quite hidden
from the world. She was never the object of public
curiosity or veneration. From outward appearances her life
seemed ordinary, but her soul lived in the heights. She was
especially chosen by God to be a *soul victim*, that is, she
was especially called to sacrifice and suffer for the
conversion of sinners. In other words, she was a victim of
Divine Love. Hers was a life of sacrifice and suffering for
the conversion of sinners and in reparation for sin.

Early Childhood

Gemma was born at Camigliano, Italy on March 12th, 1878.
She was the fourth of the eight children, and the eldest
daughter of Henry and Aurelia Galgani. Her father was a
very successful pharmacist (apothecarist). A month after
her birth, the family removed to Lucca, where she remained
the rest of her life. Sacrifice and suffering began for her at a
young age. Like all children, Gemma loved her mother
with all her little heart. Her mother was a holy and devout

---

[1] A Christian who has not taken up the vocation of ministry such as a
priest, nun, monk, deacon, etc.

Catholic, and Gemma's first lessons in Christian piety were received on her mother's knee, and it was by her mother's side in their parish church that she first learned to taste the 'hidden and unutterable sweetness of the Mass.'

'It was Mamma,' she said years afterwards, 'who, as a child, made me desire to go to Heaven.'

Death of Her Mother

It was during these tender years that her mother fell a victim to tuberculosis. Her long lingering illness, endured with saintly resignation, was made more difficult by the thought that she must soon leave her children when they most needed her care. Gemma came to know that her mother was going to the Heaven of which she had so often heard her speak, and her great wish was to go with her. Every day as she returned from school her first thought was to hurry to her mother's sickroom, fearing that her mother might have taken flight in her absence. Meanwhile the day of her Confirmation came, May 26th, 1885, and with it the first of those heavenly communications which played such a large a part in her spiritual life. During the Mass of Thanksgiving after the ceremony 'all of a sudden,' she tells us, 'a voice in my heart said to me: *'Will you give me your Mamma? 'Yes,'* I answered, *'if you will take me as well.' 'No,'* the voice replied. *'Give me your Mamma without reserve. I will take you to Heaven later.'* 'I could only answer *'Yes,'* and when Mass was over I ran home.'

It was her first great sacrifice, and it cost her bitter grief and tears; but when her mother died a few months later it was Gemma who consoled the others. Gemma was only eight years old. *'Why should we cry? Mamma is gone to Heaven.'* she said.

Shortly after her mother's death, Gemma was sent to the school of the Sisters of St. Zita in Lucca. Under the guidance and direction of the good Sisters, she acquired a greater taste for prayer, and a tender devotion to the Passion of Our Lord on which she began to meditate daily. Her love for the Mother of God was always deep and intense, the more so as she had lost her earthly mother. *'If God has taken away my mother,'* she would often say, *'He has left me His own.'* And her frequent prayer was: *'Holy Virgin, make me a Saint.'* During this time she often said the whole fifteen decades of the Rosary on her knees in the evening after her return from school, and she also began to use penances and to rise in the night to pray.

However, the devout life is oftentimes a hard struggle. And the help she needed and desired most was as yet denied her. She had long expressed the wish to make her First Communion. 'You are too young,' the parish priest had told her. 'Give me Jesus,' she would say to the Confessor or the Sisters, 'and you will see how good I shall be: I will not sin again, I shall be quite changed.' But the custom of the time was against Communion at so early an age, and she was ten years old before permission was finally granted, and only granted by special exception. 'There is no alternative,' the Confessor declared, 'but to admit her to Communion or see her die of grief.' We can only imagine the angelic fervor with which she received her Lord for the first time on the Feast of the Sacred Heart, June 17th 1887.

'I feel a fire burning here,' she said to one of her fellow friends afterwards, pointing to her breast. 'Do you feel like that?' She did not imagine that there was anything exceptional in her own experience. Her life afterwards was a constant growth in union with Jesus. 'Gemma is good for nothing,' she would say, 'but Gemma and Jesus can do all things.'

Gemma's school life was brought to an end by a painful illness. An injury to her foot which she made light of resulted in a severe and painful infection, and she was forced to remain bedridden for some months. An operation was necessary, but she refused an anesthetic, and with eyes fixed on the crucifix suffered the excruciating pain with little but a moan or two. The doctors were amazed and edified by her courage and endurance.

Restored to health, she now took her place in the home to do the duties that naturally fall to the eldest daughter in a motherless family. During this time she kept quite busy, for it was a large household. In the intervals she busied herself in making altar linen and vestments for the church or clothing for the poor. However, her activities were not confined to the home. She would often gather the poor children of the neighborhood together for religious instruction. She frequently visited the sick in hospitals, bringing them little material comforts but especially 'comforting them with thoughts of God.' Her charity to the poor and sick went almost to the point of extravagance. Every time she went out, she would ask her father for money to give in charity, and if sometimes he refused she would coax permission to take bread or whatever she could lay her hands on at the moment.

Her home duties and her pressing concern for others were in no sense an obstacle to the growth of her interior life. Rather the contrary: her busy life of active charity drew its inspiration from her life of prayer and union with God. When she was most occupied with external things, she seemed to those around her wholly absorbed in God. 'Her life was one continual prayer,' says a priest who knew her well, 'and her prayer-book was the Crucifix.' The thought of the sufferings of Christ never left her, and it was in those days, as she tells us, she 'began to feel a growing desire to love Jesus Crucified with all her heart, and together with this a longing to help Him in His sufferings.' She was especially drawn and devoted to the Passion of our Lord. 'O Jesus,' she prayed, 'I wish to follow You whatever it may cost me of suffering—to follow You fervently—I wish to suffer for You.'

Grave Illness

God was not long in answering her prayer, for it was at this time that she was diagnosed with spinal tuberculosis (or possibly spinal meningitis). She had felt symptoms for a while, but her pious repugnance to medical examination made her conceal it until she found herself bedridden. Her pitiful condition, and the patience and sweetness with which she suffered, drew those who knew her to her bedside. One of these brought her the *Life of Venerable Gabriel Possenti*, who was known for his sanctity and miracles though not yet canonized at that time. Gemma at first took little interest in the Life, but having once invoked Brother Gabriel's name in a distressing temptation with instant effect, she then read the book several times and thus developed a special devotion to him. Not long afterwards, he appeared to her amidst her grave illness, speaking words of consolation and encouragement.

Miraculous Cure

In February 1899, the doctors pronounced her case hopeless, and she received the Last Sacraments. Her Confessor since childhood, Monsignor Giovanni Volpi, auxiliary Bishop of Lucca and afterwards Bishop of Arezzo, visited her on February 19th and suggested she should make a novena to St Margaret Mary Alacoque for her recovery. Twice she began the novena, but forgot to continue it. What then followed may be best told in her own words:

'On the 23rd February I began it for the third time, or rather had meant to begin it, for it was now within a few minutes of midnight, when I heard the clink of a rosary beads and felt a hand laid on my forehead. A voice said the Our Father, Hail Mary, and Gloria nine times in succession. I hardly answered, I was so weak. Then the voice said: *'Do you wish to be cured? Yes, you will be cured. Pray with faith to the Sacred Heart of Jesus. I will come every evening till the end of the novena and we shall pray together to the Sacred Heart.'*

'And what of Blessed Margaret Mary?' I asked.

'Repeat the Gloria three times in her honor.'

It was the Passionist, St Gabriel Possenti, who had appeared and encouraged her.

'He came every evening and we recited the prayers together. The novena was to end on the first Friday of March. Early that morning I received Holy Communion. Oh, what happy moments I passed with Jesus. He, too, asked me, *'Do you wish to be cured?'* My emotion was so great that I could not speak, but in my heart I answered, 'Whatever You will, O Jesus!' The grace was granted. I was cured. I rose from bed. Those in the house were crying for joy. I too was pleased, but not so much that I had been cured as that Jesus had chosen me for His child. For that morning before He left me, He had said: *'My child, the grace you have received this morning will be followed by many others still greater.'*

Gemma's cure was complete and permanent. Her illness had lasted more than a year and had brought her to death's door, but afterwards her health was perfectly normal.

Her first thought after her recovery was one she had long hoped for—that of entering a convent. Circumstances up to this point had made it impossible to realize, but now her way seemed clear. Several religious communities in Lucca would gladly have accepted her, and even encouraged her hopes. But ecclesiastical authority was slow to believe in the permanence of her sudden cure from such a dangerous disease, and also her extraordinary mystical experiences were known to the local Bishop. So, to her great sorrow, Gemma found the convent doors regretfully but firmly barred against her.

Meanwhile, her spiritual life continued to grow in intensity and fervor; her union with God became more intimate, and her soul began to be visited with divine communications of the most extraordinary and exalted kind. She had been accustomed even during her illness to make the Holy Hour in honor of the agony of Jesus in Gethsemane. In gratitude for her recovery, she now promised the Sacred Heart of Jesus that she would recite the Holy Hour every Thursday night— a promise she kept for the remainder of her life. It was during this Holy Hour that Jesus began to pour into her soul those marvelous and extraordinary graces which made of her life a martyrdom of love. Her first experience on this Holy Thursday she thus described to her spiritual director—

'I spent the whole hour praying and weeping for my sins. Feeling weak, I sat down. The sorrow continued, but after a little I felt rapt in recollection. Shortly afterwards I suddenly lost the use of my senses. I tried to get up and lock the door of my room. Where was I? I found myself in the presence of Jesus Crucified, blood flowing from His wounds. The sight filled me with pain. I lowered my eyes and made the Sign of the Cross: I felt great peace of mind, but still intense sorrow for my sins. I had not the courage to look at Jesus. I bent down with forehead to the ground and remained so for several hours— when I came to myself the wounds of Jesus were so impressed on my mind that they have never since left it.'

The vision filled Gemma with a new horror for sin and with an intense desire to suffer with Jesus and to become a victim for the salvation of souls. The desire was to be gratified in a way she little expected. One morning after Holy Communion she heard the voice of Jesus say to her, *'Courage Gemma, I wait for you on Calvary where you are soon going.'*

Gemma Receives the Stigmata

The meaning of the words was soon made plain. A few days later, on Thursday, June 8th, the eve of the Feast of the Sacred Heart, when she began as usual to make the Holy Hour, she felt a piercing sorrow for her sins such as she had never experienced, and a peculiarly vivid sense of the sufferings of Jesus. Suddenly she was rapt in ecstasy and found herself in the presence of her heavenly Mother and her Guardian Angel. The angel made her repeat an act of contrition, and Mary comforted her with the assurance that her sins were forgiven, and told her she was to receive a great grace through the love of Jesus. 'Then'—they are Gemma's own words—

'she opened her mantle and covered me with it. At the same moment Jesus appeared with His wounds open: but instead of blood, flames as it were of fire seemed to issue from them. In an instant those flames touched my hands and feet and heart. I felt as if I were dying and should have fallen to the floor, had not my Mother supported me under her mantle. I remained in that position some hours. Then she kissed my forehead, the vision disappeared, and I found myself on my knees alone: but I still felt intense pain in my hands, feet, and heart. I rose to go to bed, but I found that blood was flowing from the places where I had the pain. I covered them as well as I could and got into bed with the help of my Guardian Angel. Next morning I found it difficult to go to Holy Communion. I put on a pair of gloves to hide my hands. But I could scarcely stand, and felt every moment that I should die. Those pains continued until 3:00 p.m. on Friday, the Feast of the Sacred Heart.'

Apart from her confusion and distress at such a sinner being so favored, Gemma's only thought seems to have been like that which occurred to her after her First Communion *when she felt a fire burning in her heart and also that it was a common experience with those whom Jesus had chosen for His own.*[1] She began to make timid inquiries among her friends during the day, but only succeeded in mystifying them without obtaining any information. At last, feeling that she must confide in someone, as the blood continued to flow, she went to her aunt, and holding up her hands, said with the simplicity of a child, *'Aunt, see what Jesus has done to me.'* The good woman was struck dumb with amazement, but as little understood the meaning of the strange phenomenon as Gemma herself.

The phenomenon was repeated regularly every Thursday evening, beginning about 11:00 p.m. and lasting until 3:00 p.m. in the afternoon of Friday. Gemma seemed to pass through all the phases of the Passion, and bore in her body all the marks of Christ's physical sufferings: not only the wounds in hands, feet, and side, but the punctures of the crown of thorns, the marks of the scourging, the wound on the shoulder caused by the weight of the Cross, all accompanied with the most excruciating pain. Throughout those hours she engaged in loving conversations and colloquies with Jesus in a low voice, often tenderly pleading for mercy for sinners and offering herself as a victim in expiation for their sins.

For some time Gemma kept these extraordinary occurrences a secret even from her Confessor: partly through her extreme humility and partly through the difficulty of explaining them in the confessional. A few weeks after they began, however, a mission was given by the Passionist Fathers in Lucca which Gemma attended.

---

[1] emphasis of the editor of the present edition

After the general Communion on the last day of the mission, she heard an interior voice which said: *'You shall be a daughter of My Passion, and a favorite daughter: one of these shall be a father to you: go and make everything known to them.'*

She found a prudent and sympathetic adviser in one of the missioners, who communicated with Mgr. Volpi, her Confessor, with the result that the Passionist Father Germanus was ultimately appointed her spiritual director. Mgr. Volpi was perplexed and doubtful about the authenticity of Gemma's extraordinary mystical experiences. The mission Father and those whom he consulted were equally at a loss. Father Germanus, a priest of large experience and of a dry and scientific turn of mind, was frankly skeptical when first consulted by Mgr. Volpi, and he initially declined to have anything to do with Gemma, and advised him to make his penitent follow the common spiritual path. It was only after considerable pressure that he was induced to visit her. After a searching and thorough investigation, however, he came to recognize in her an elect soul, 'a true Gem of the Sacred Heart of Jesus,' and remained her spiritual director for the rest of her life. After her death he wrote a first-hand biography of Gemma entitled *'The Life of Saint Gemma Galgani.'*

Gemma Moves into the Giannini Home

At this time Gemma's father died, leaving the family destitute, and she was then obligated to live with one of her aunts. Gemma was 19 years old at that time. 'It is good to hide the secrets of the King,' and one of Gemma's chief anxieties was to keep secret the great things God had done to her from the eyes of outsiders. It was soon evident that in her aunt's house this was impossible. The younger members of the family were curious. Not one was sympathetic; things began to be talked of outside, and much of what was said was not kind. Gemma was frequently rapt in ecstasy even in the course of her daily occupations, and was thus at the mercy of those nearby who did not understand such extraordinary graces. She had to suffer much in consequence. At length, through the influence of the Passionist Fathers, she was received into the home of their benefactors the Giannini family; a well-known family in Lucca, first as an occasional guest, then finally as an adopted daughter. The household consisted of the father and mother with eleven children, and an aunt named Cecilia, who already knew and admired Gemma and was to become a adopted 'mother' to her.

The overall quality and character of this family may be seen from a sentence or two of the father's (Matteo Giannini) evidence in the *Process for the Beatification of Gemma* where, telling of her influence in his home, he speaks of 'my five sons who are a great consolation to me. They go to Holy Communion every day and are much engaged in the field of Catholic Action. Of my daughters, five are nuns, one has remained at home,[1] and one is married.'

Daily Life

In the Giannini home Gemma was sheltered from the prying eyes of the world and from the reputation for uncommon sanctity which she so dreaded. Her life in the Giannini household may surprise those who perhaps imagine that a life of exalted and continuous prayer must be one of inaction. For it was a life of constant and useful activity. Signor Giannini, just quoted, summed it up by saying, 'Gemma was never idle.'

'At first when she came to us,' says her adopted mother Cecilia, 'she used to crochet, but she preferred knitting or

---

[1] Gemma, we assume.

mending stockings, because I believe it permitted her to keep more recollected. It kept her busy, for she mended for the whole family. She was always ready to do whatever there was to do. She was never unoccupied.' A priest who lived with the family and saw her at her daily duties could not help admiring 'her spirit of recollection[1] and union with God. Even in the midst of the most distracting domestic occupations, she always seemed as if absorbed in God and in continual meditation. But this did not hinder her from attending with great care to whatever she was doing.'

Another duty she especially coveted was the care of the sick. 'She always looked after those who were ill in the house with the greatest care and attention, and in all things showing the greatest kindness and charity; and all this she did for the love of God.'

However, few indeed would have suspected from Gemma's ordinary external life the sublime spiritual heights to which she was raised. Her simplicity and humility threw an effective veil over the secrets of her interior life. A priest, who frequently visited the Giannini family and knew her well, was unaware of her extraordinary holiness until her death revealed it. 'Her modesty and simplicity,' he tells us, 'made a most pleasing impression on me. And though I often came in contact with her, I could not find in her the smallest imperfection. Her words were few, and in answer only to questions asked of her. I never heard her speak of herself. But while knowing well that she had a most delicate conscience and a beautiful soul, all intent on loving God, I should never have thought that she was so far advanced in sanctity.'

Father Germanus tells us that if there was a virtue characteristic of Gemma, it was her evangelical simplicity.[2] It distinguished her from childhood and accompanied her

---

[1] contemplation
[2] A simplicity that in essence preached the 'good message' (euaggelion) or 'god-spell' of eternal life.

all along her ascent to the summits of the supernatural life. She could not bear to think or speak to the detriment of anyone. 'You would need a wrench,' a witness said in the Processes,[1] 'to draw a word from her regarding others, even when the information was necessary, if it had to be an unfavorable word.' She was frequently rapt in ecstasy during the day, but on returning to herself, went on with her work apparently unconscious of any interruption. And after the long weekly ecstasy 'she would rise as if nothing had happened, wash away the stains of the blood which had flowed so profusely, draw down her sleeves to cover the large scars on her hands, and believing that no one had noticed her, would return to the other members of the family and take her part in the work of the day.'

It was her simplicity that led her to think at first that her mystical experiences were common with all those who wish to love God. And when she realized that they were exceptional, she was haunted by the fear that she might be deceived or a deceiver. She had heard of such cases from those least qualified to deal with her. She had even heard a whisper of the ugly word 'hysteria.' And she would ask her director:

'Am I to believe it is Jesus, or the Devil, or my own imagination? I am ignorant, and I may be deceived. What would become of me if I were the victim of delusion? You know I do not wish these things. I only wish Jesus to be pleased with me.' Or again, 'Can it be that I am a deceiver? If I am, I shall lose my soul. I should like you to explain what a deceiver is, for I do not want to deceive anyone.'

She found her only consolation in absolute obedience to her Confessor and her spiritual director: 'Oh, what consolation my heart finds in obedience! It fills me with a calm I cannot explain. Dear obedience! Source of all my

---

[1] Led by a priest called 'the Devil's Advocate' who strenuously researches the life of every person alleged to be a saint to see if this is in fact true.

peace.'

Gemma and the Conversion of Sinners

Gemma's whole life indeed was one long uninterrupted sacrifice of the most heroic kind. To a worldly mind, such a life of suffering may seem horrible, and even tragic. There is one secret which fully explains it. From her earliest childhood, the contemplation of Jesus Crucified filled her with a sense of her own sinfulness and a desire to atone for it, and then to be associated with Him in His sufferings and to share them in reparation for the sins of the world. To win souls for Jesus through prayer and suffering was the one passion of her life. Even as a child at school, her teacher says, 'Gemma suffered because sin was committed. I remember that when she was quite a small child she grieved if any of her companions acted wrongly. She prayed much, but especially for poor sinners, and offered for them such mortifications as a child can perform.' It was the feature of her life which the witnesses to her heroic sanctity repeatedly singled out as characteristic of her. Thus, some of the witnesses have stated:

'She was especially attracted to pray for poor sinners.'

'She was much afflicted by the thought of the sins committed in the world and she often offered herself to God on behalf of sinners.'

'She would gladly have gone through the world to work for the extension of Christ's kingdom by converting pagans, heretics, and sinners.'

'The sins of mankind and the insults these offences offered to Jesus were an acute and constant source of suffering to Gemma.'

She was often heard in ecstasy pleading for sinners and even offering her life for them. 'What do You wish, O Jesus? My life? It is Yours. I have already offered it to You. Will You be pleased if I offer it again as a victim in expiation for my sins and those of all sinners? If I had a hundred lives I would give every one of them to You!'

And in her letters she frequently returns to the same thought:

'What is sweeter than to be filled with the thought of Jesus and to kneel before that Divine Victim of love and sorrow—a Victim for my sins, for my salvation and for the salvation of souls?'

'I should willingly give every drop of my blood to please Him and to prevent sinners from offending Him.'

'I shall be satisfied only when I am a victim—and may it be soon—to make reparation for my innumerable sins and for the sins of all the world.'

She did not confine herself to intercession for sinners in general, but almost constantly 'carried on her shoulders,' as she would say, some obstinate sinner for whom she was asked to pray. And endless conversions were wrought by her prayers, from the dying man who refused to receive the Last Sacraments who was converted by her prayers as a child at school, to the notorious sinner of Lucca whose conversion was announced to her the day before she died. Her sufferings were not meaningless, nor merely a personal discipline: they were the instrument of a great apostolate[1] for the sanctification of souls, and especially for the conversion of sinners, that drew all its inspiration and all its virtue from her continual union with Jesus Crucified.

Desires to Become a Nun, but is Denied

She had never lost her childhood's desire of entering a convent. And from the time she first met the Passionists and heard of the Passionist nuns, she felt that her place was with them. There was a convent of the order at Corneto, Italy, some two hundred miles from Lucca, and after asking advice, she determined to go there for a course of spiritual exercises and ask admission. She met with a decided refusal, worded in no very genial terms,[2] from a Reverend Mother who had heard about Gema's illness and cure, and also the extraordinary graces that surrounded her life, and was therefore convinced that such a mystic (or possible hysteric?) would not be suitable for their contemplative Community. It was a bitter disappointment to Gemma, but she bore it bravely and patiently. Subsequent efforts were made in her behalf by her Confessor Mgr. Volpi and her spiritual director Father Germanus, but without any effect. Gemma began as far as she could to lead the life of a Passionist nun outside the cloister. She had already made a vow of chastity during her serious illness, and to this she now added, with her Confessor's approval, the vows of poverty and obedience. She wore the Sign of the Passion on her heart underneath her clothing, and recited the Divine Office daily like the Passionist nuns in choir. And she never lost the hope, till near the end of her life, of joining them, if not at Corneto, then elsewhere.

Her hope to become a Passionist nun was eventually

---

[1] The taking of a truth to those who need it, from *apostellein*, meaning 'to send off.'
[2] worded harshly

realized after her death. In her first letter to Father Germanus, before she had yet met him, she predicted in minute detail the establishment of a convent of Passionist nuns at Lucca. There was no thought of such a project at the time, but a year or two later it began to be talked of. Gemma was filled with enthusiasm, and began to pray and to use all the influence in her power to hasten the coming of the nuns to Lucca. The difficulties in the way seemed at times insurmountable, but she was never disheartened. During the last year of her life it was her constant thought and the constant object of her prayers. She even searched Lucca more than once for a suitable site and interested herself in the material funds necessary for the foundation. She still had hopes of finding her vocation in the new convent. But towards the end she made the sacrifice even of these, if only the work on which she had set her heart might be accomplished:

'I no longer ask to enter a convent. Jesus has the habit of a Passionist nun waiting for me at the gates of Heaven. Let me die so that the Passionist convent may be established.'

She assured those who were losing heart that the foundation would be begun after her death and completed in the year of the Beatification of St Gabriel. Her words, contrary to all expectation, were verified by the events. Two years after Gemma's death, the first little group of Passionist Sisters came to Lucca, and though they met with many obstacles and disappointments, a full community took possession of the new convent in 1908, just two months after St Gabriel was beatified. Pope Pius X had already blessed the project, and, in words which would have brought joy to the heart of Gemma, assigned as the special object of the community that 'of offering themselves as victims to Our Lord for the spiritual and temporal needs of the Church and of the Sovereign Pontiff.'

Today the Passionist convent in Lucca continues to flourish. Gemma's body reposes near the altar in the little chapel, and the nuns venerate her as their foundress and the patroness of their work. 'The Passionist nuns would not accept me,' she had said, 'but for all that I wish to be one of them, and I shall be with them when I am dead.' So was Gemma's wish fulfilled at last. 'If for reasons independent of her will,' writes a companion of hers now a Carmelite nun, 'Gemma never wore the Passionist habit, she was none the less a true Passionist. She was a Passionist in soul, and she had the spirit of the Passionists. The Order has made her its own. Her convent has been established for years and continues to flourish exceedingly.' The same thought was expressed by Benedict XV in the decree introducing the Cause of her Beatification: 'The pious virgin, Gemma Galgani, if not by habit and profession, undoubtedly by desire and affection is rightly numbered among the religious children of St Paul of the Cross.' And Pius XI in proclaiming her heroic sanctity congratulated 'the sons and daughters of St Paul of the Cross on the possession of this true gem of sanctity who would be an additional honor to their Congregation.' Gemma had once described herself as 'wandering like a soul that had gone astray': her long cherished vocation was at last realized and certainly not many vocations have cost such a painful sacrifice.

Gemma had offered herself to God as a victim in expiation of the sins of men, and her offering had been accepted. Up to this point she had shared in all the sufferings of Jesus except one—the last and greatest, the agony, sorrow, and destitution of His last hours on the Cross. Terribly as she had to this point suffered in soul and body, her suffering had been in secret, and her life was more like Gethsemane than Calvary. After her miraculous cure, her health had been perfectly normal, and no one would have suspected that the strong, healthy girl was enduring the tortures of a living martyrdom. But the moment came when her sufferings could no longer be hidden: it was the immolation[1] of the victim.

Final Illness

At Pentecost, 1902, she was suddenly stricken with a mysterious illness which lasted, with one short interval, for the remaining nine months of her life. She could not taste any food, her body was torn with the most violent pains, and she was reduced to a skeleton. At first she managed to drag herself to church for Mass and Holy Communion, with the help of her adopted mother and friend Cecilia, but this consolation soon had to be abandoned due to her deteriorating health. Doctors were called in, but disagreed in their diagnosis and for the most part confessed themselves baffled by the mysterious nature of her disease. The pains which racked her body without ceasing were aggravated by furious assaults of the Devil on her body and her soul, so horrendous and continuous that she imagined herself possessed and begged to be exorcized. Her heroic life, all the virtues she had practiced, all the divine favors she had received, were now represented to her[2] as an accumulation of hypocrisy and deceit. And during all those months of suffering, no ray of divine consolation reached her heart. She continued to pray unceasingly, calling on Jesus and Mary to be with her in this hour of bitter dereliction, and outwardly preserved a serene and unruffled calmness. Of her bodily pains she never complained but once, when she murmured, 'My Jesus, it is more than I can bear': but when the Sister in attendance on her reminded her that with God's grace it is possible to bear all things, she never used the words again. On the contrary, when the

---

[1] burnt offering
[2] by demonic forces

Sister once asked her 'If you had your choice which would it be: to go at once to Heaven and cease to suffer or to remain here and suffer for the glory of God?'

'Better to suffer,' she said, 'than go to Heaven when the pain is for Jesus and His glory.'

One of the religious nursing Sisters from the Order of St Camillus who cared for Gemma during her last illness stated 'We have cared for a good many sick people, but we have never seen anything like this!'

Holy Death

One last consolation remained to Gemma, and of this she was soon to be deprived. Pitiable as was her condition, she was at least in the midst of affectionate friends. Some of the doctors, however, were of opinion that her disease was tuberculosis, and Father Germanus was anxious that the children of the family should not be exposed to the danger of infection. It was decided to remove Gemma, much to the disappointment of the Giannini family, who offered strong opposition. Some months passed indeed before they could be induced to consent to it. At last a compromise was made and a room was rented across the street from which communication could be held with the Giannini home by means of a bell fixed to a cord stretched across an intervening courtyard. Here Gemma was removed on February 24th 1903, making her last sacrifice with a calm resignation that astonished even those who knew her best. At this point she could very well say, 'I have made a sacrifice of everything; nothing now remains for me but to prepare for death.'

Death was not far off. Some two months later, on Good Friday; she entered with outstretched arms into a prolonged ecstasy, nailed, as she said, with Jesus to the Cross. Those who saw her suffering throughout that day and the following night knew that the end was at hand. On Holy

Saturday a priest was called and gave her Extreme Unction, and then Gemma was left to taste the full bitterness of the desolation of Jesus on Calvary.[1] The end came peacefully when, with a look of seraphic[2] joy on her face, she gave up her pure soul to God an hour after midday on Holy Saturday, April 11th 1903. Her countenance was so beautiful and peaceful that those present found it difficult to convince themselves that she was actually dead.

Gemma Galgani was beatified by Pope Pius XI on May 14th 1933, and canonized[3] by Pope Pius XII on Ascension Thursday, May 2nd 1940. Among the vast multitude that filled St Peter's[4] on the day of her Canonization were thirteen hundred of the citizens of Lucca headed by their Archbishop. Many of them had known her, including the numerous members of the Giannini family which had so devotedly befriended her. There, too, was her youngest sister Angelina sitting by the side of the nun of St. Zita who had taught Gemma as a child and guided her first steps in the path of heroic sanctity.

The feast of St Gemma is April 11th (and also May 16th for those in the Passionist Congregation).

---

[1] Psalm 22; Matthew 27:46
[2] like a Seraph; angelic
[3] made a saint
[4] Basilica of St Peter (The Vatican, Rome)

Afterword by the Publisher

It may be noted by anyone reading the life of St. Gemma, or the life of any other saint, canonized or not, that holy lives such as theirs are first gifts to them through the grace of our Creator who loves them, but secondly serve as gifts of light and power to Christianity as well as its counterfeit known as Christendom—which has always been represented by organized religion and a variety of denominations beginning with the unnecessary cliques who claimed they followed Paul or Apollo to Roman Catholicism to Eastern Orthodoxy to the many and varied versions of Protestantism which continue to sprout for a season and then wither away.

Saints are the lights and salt of Christ for a dark and insipid world, their lives serving to minister the power of our Creator's love and forgiveness wherever they are placed inside religious circles, or outside of them, and whether they are ever recognized as saints or not. A tree is known by its fruit, not by what grove it grows in.

~ Hagios Publications

Made in United States
North Haven, CT
24 April 2022

18527877R00082